Mastering Applications in the Real World
Discipline-Specific Projects for Microsoft® Office

Steven Freund
University of Central Florida

Debi Griggs
Bellevue Community College

Debra Gross
The Ohio State University

Luis A. Lopez
St. Philip's College

Brian M. Morgan
Marshall University

Blaine P. Robertson
Brigham Young University - Idaho

Amanda J. Salinas
St. Philip's College

Rebekah Tidwell
Lee University and Tidwell Consulting

With special thanks to reviewers:
Risa Blair, Angley College
Zona Gale, Santa Fe Community College
Vickee Stedham, St. Petersburg College
Andrea Wachter, Point Park College

THOMSON
COURSE TECHNOLOGY

Australia • Canada • Mexico • Singapore • Spain • United Kingdom • United States • Japan

THOMSON

™

COURSE TECHNOLOGY

**Mastering Applications in the Real World:
Discipline-Specific Projects for Microsoft® Office**

is published by Course Technology.

Managing Editor:
Rachel Crapser

Product Manager:
Karen Stevens

Associate Product Manager:
Brianna Germain

Editorial Assistants:
Emilie Perreault, Abbey Reider

Marketing Manager:
Rachel Valente

Production Editors:
Kristen Guevara, Philippa Lehar

Composition:
GEX Publishing Services

Text Designers:
Abby Scholz, GEX Publishing Services

Cover Designers:
Steve Deschene, Julie Malone

CONTENTS

COMFORT COMMUNITY COLLEGE HUMAN RESOURCES

PROBLEM STATEMENT

Comfort Community College (CCC) is a relatively new college having opened its doors just six years ago. Throughout its short history the CCC Human Resources Department has developed documents that describe its procedures and policies. These documents have been developed on an as-needed basis; however, now the department director sees a need to consolidate these documents into a Human Resources Manual that will have a consistent look and be easy to maintain. The director has asked you to create the manual using existing documents and to convert the final document to Web pages for posting on the college intranet.

AVAILABLE DATA

Data Files: **hr manual.doc; leave.doc; benefits.doc; payroll.doc; grievance.doc; paygrades.xls**

Web Sites: For relevant Web sites, visit the Student Online Companion at **www.course.com/downloads/sites/projects**

TASKS

A. Accept Reviewer Changes and Comments

You have been instructed by your supervisor to accept the changes currently identified in the HR Manual document. These changes are based on reviewer comments and changes made by the director of human resources.

1. Open **hr manual.doc** and save it as **hr manual sol.doc**.

2. Accept each of the changes and delete the comments.

B. Create a Master Document

There are several documents that need to be incorporated into the Human Resources Manual. It is very likely that more documents will be added in the future. To better manage this manual you will convert it into a master document and insert the existing documents as subdocuments. Future documents can be easily added to the manual, and the subdocuments can also be modified independently of the manual.

1. Convert the **hr manual sol** document to a master document by adding the following documents as subdocuments in the order listed. Insert these documents at the end of the document.

   - **leave.doc**
   - **benefits.doc**
   - **payroll.doc**
   - **grievance.doc**

2. The Work Rules section in the master document will expand as more rules are defined by HR staff. To make this section easier to maintain, convert it to a subdocument. This makes it into a separate document when it is saved.

3. Change the **Payroll** subdocument so that it becomes part of the master document.

4. Change the **Work Rules**, **Promotions**, and **Safety** headings so that they have an Outline Level of 1.

5. Change the Outline view to Show Level 3. The document should look similar to that shown in Figure 1.

FIGURE 1   Outline View Level 3

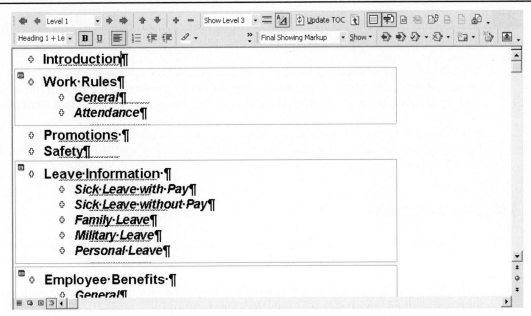

C. Structure the Document

The HR Manual will be printed for distribution to college departments. It should be organized for ease of access, and it should be clearly identified.

1. Add section numbers so that the headings are numbered in Arabic numerals in the form of an outline.
   - First-level headings should be labeled with a number such as 1, 2, 3, etc.
   - Subheadings should include the top-level number plus numbers indicating they are subheadings. For example, second-level headings would be labeled 1.1, 1.2, 1.3, etc.
   - Third-level headings should be labeled 1.1.1, 1.1.2, 1.1.3, etc.

2. Give every page the following title: **Comfort Community College Human Resources Manual**, except the first page of the manual.

3. Provide the page number and the section name (using first-level section headings) centered at the bottom of each page, except the first.

4. Add a ½ inch gutter to allow for binding when the document is printed.

D. Create Hyperlinks

The director of human resources would like to have a list of useful links to Web sites with information related to human resources management and has directed you to a Web site where the links are listed.

1. Add a new section at the end of the master document with a list of URL links and descriptions, using "Web Resources" as the section heading. The list of relevant links is listed on the Student Online Companion.

E. Embed Graphics

In an effort to make the HR Manual more user-friendly, you decide to add several graphic images including an AutoShape and clip art.

1. Add clip art images to two of the main sections in the manual. Each clip art image should be placed right after the section heading, to the left of the section's first paragraph. Use clip art that is available with Word, and make sure the images relate to an office environment.

2. Add an AutoShape in the form of a banner to the beginning of the document. Move the college name inside the banner, and center the document title, **Human Resources Manual**, below the banner. Format the banner in a professional manner.

F. Add a Watermark

The HR director requests that the printed manual include a watermark to indicate that it is only for use by employees of the college. This watermark should appear on every page.

1. Add a text watermark that reads **Staff Use Only**. The watermark font should be Arial, with a size of 44 and it should be positioned diagonally. Accept the default color of light gray and Semitransparent.

G. Insert an Excel Spreadsheet

Another HR staff member has given you an Excel spreadsheet that she maintains. This spreadsheet lists the different pay grades that apply to nonfaculty positions at Comfort Community College. You are to include this information in the HR Manual.

1. Add a second-level heading to the Payroll section. Use **Pay Grades** as the text for this heading. Then enter the following paragraph below the heading:

   Staff pay grades are provided for nonfaculty positions. These pay grades are subject to change. Check with the human resources office for the most up-to-date pay grade schedule.

2. Insert the **paygrades.xls** worksheet after the paragraph. Do not link the inserted object to the worksheet file.

3. Add a caption to the pay grade table. The caption should be **Figure 1**.

4. Insert a cross-reference to this figure between the words "provided" and "for" in the paragraph entered in Step 1 above. Add the word **in** before the cross-reference. The result should read, "Staff pay grades are provided in Figure 1 for nonfaculty positions."

H. Create a Table of Contents

To make it easier for employees to locate specific sections of the manual, add a table of contents based on the section headers. The table of contents can be easily updated as more documents are created and added to the manual.

1. Add the word **Contents** after "Human Resources Manual" on the first page. Below "Contents," insert the table of contents. Make sure the section numbers for the headings match those you set up in Task C.

I. Convert the Document to Web Pages

Now that you have completed the HR Manual, you are to convert it to a Web page to make it more easily accessible to all employees. You first convert all of the subdocuments to be part of the master document. This makes all of the content part of one Web page.

1. Save the master document, **hr manual sol.doc**. Then convert each of its subdocuments so that they become part of the master document. You want just one document with all the content before converting it to a Web page. Make sure to left-align the title, Human Resources Manual, for improved readability on a Web browser. Now save this version of the document as **hr manual sol2.doc**.

2. Convert **hr manual sol2.doc** into a Web page with the name **hrmanual.htm**. If necessary, change the Web page title to **Human Resources Manual**. Be sure to view the Web page in your Web browser.

PROJECT RESULTS |

Upon completion, you should have the following files:

    hr manual sol.doc
    Work Rules.doc
    hr manual sol2.doc
    hrmanual.htm
    hrmanual_files folder

ED'S FEED STORE

PROBLEM STATEMENT

Ed's Feed Store sells agricultural products to many of the farms in and around Bandera County. Many of Ed Garza's customers buy feed supplies in bulk and pay the store on a monthly basis. To keep track of his customers' accounts, Ed has developed an Access database which he updates regularly. This database includes customer name and address information as well as current account balance. Ed also maintains an Excel spreadsheet to keep track of current feed prices.

Ed has hired you to create billing statements that will be mailed to his customers. He would like the billing statements to include customer information and account balance. He would also like for each statement to include a current list of feed prices based on the Excel spreadsheet he maintains.

AVAILABLE DATA

Data files: **Customers.txt; feed.xls**

The customer list has already been exported from Access into a text file. The current feed price list is an Excel spreadsheet.

TASKS

A. Create the Billing Statement Form Letter

Ed has asked you to create a billing statement that contains the store's name and address. One statement will be printed for each customer with that customer's name, address, phone, and account balance. You need to combine the customer information (already exported from Access) with the Word document to produce a billing statement for each customer.

The statement contains a short message from the store followed by a table with the customer information and account balance. If the account balance is zero, a message is printed indicating the account is up to date. The table should be formatted to make the information easier to read.

1. Create a new Word document and save it as **billing.doc**. Use Times New Roman with a font size of 12 for the text, unless otherwise instructed.

2. Type the following store name and address at the top of the document. Add a bottom border to the last line of the address.

   Ed's Feed Store
   115 Farm Rd 2
   Bandera, TX 78233

3. Type the following message two lines after the store address:

   At Ed's Feed store we value your business and will do all we can to provide the materials and supplies for your home and business agricultural needs.

   Thank you!
   Ed Garza

4. Skip two lines and then type the following lines. Insert the current date in the first line making sure that the date is updated automatically each time the document is opened.

   Customer Statement as of (*insert current date*)

   *Balance due at the end of the month.
   If you have any questions, please contact us at 533-3333.

B. Emphasize the Store Name

Ed has asked you make the store name larger than the other text so that it stands out.

1. Use WordArt to format the store name. Format the store name as shown in Figure 1.

FIGURE 1   Results of Word Art

C. Format Customer Information

Ed wants the customer information to have a professional appearance. He would also like the account balance to stand out from the rest of the information. You decide to use a table to present the customer information. Using a table makes it easier to format the information. You will merge the data in a later step.

1. Insert a table on a new line right after the line with the current date. The table should have five columns and three rows. The headers for the columns are **Name**, **Address**, **Phone**, **City**, and **Balance**. Place an asterisk to the right of the header **Balance**.

2. Format the table using a Table AutoFormat option so that different shading is used for the header row and the data rows to give the table a professional appearance.

D. Link to Current Feed Prices

Ed maintains a spreadsheet with current feed prices. He keeps it up to date as these prices may change monthly. As a service to his customers, he wants to provide this information along with the billing statement.

You decide to link the Excel spreadsheet to the billing statement. This way when Ed updates the table, the billing statements will also contain current information.

1. Add the following line after the line with the store phone number:

   Current feed prices provided for your information. Prices valid though the end of this month.

2. In the next line, link the **feed.xls** file.

3. Format the worksheet so that the data in each column is visible. Also, format the heading row so that the headers, **Type of Feed**, **Last Month**, and **This Month**, are bold. Change the header cells so that they are shaded with a gold color.

E. Add a Chart

In addition to the Excel spreadsheet data, Ed wants to add value in his billing statement by focusing on a different type of feed each month. This month he wants to include a chart showing a comparison of the flaxseed prices between last month and this month.

1. Add a chart below the spreadsheet data. Format the chart as shown in Figure 2. Title the chart **Flaxseed Price Comparison**.

FIGURE 2   Flaxseed Price Comparison Chart

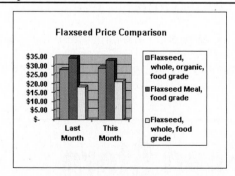

2. If necessary, format the billing statement so that it all fits on a single page.

F. Generate a Billing Letter for Each Customer

Since a billing statement will be created for each of Ed's customers, and the customer information is in a text file, you need to merge the two files. You use the Word Mail Merge Wizard to accomplish this. Specify the mail merge data source as the **Customers.txt** file. Then specify which data source fields are inserted into the billing statement document.

1. Start the Mail Merge Wizard.

2. Specify Letters as the document type and use the current document, **billing.doc**, as the starting document.

3. To select recipients, use the **Customers.txt** file. Make sure to select all of the customers in the file.

4. In the billing statement, insert the following fields in the second row of the table under each of the columns:

   FirstName and **LastName** fields in the Name column
   BillingAddress in the Address column
   PhoneNumber in the Phone column
   City in the City column

5. In the third row of the table, insert a field labeled **Balance** in the Balance column. Make this field bold with a font size of 14.

6. Add a Word field below the Balance field to print "Account is up to date." if the balance is zero. If the balance is not zero, do not print anything below the balance.

7. Preview the letters to see the billing statements created for each of the customers.

G. Edit Customer List

In previewing the letters, you notice that the statements are not in alphabetical order by customer last name as Ed had requested. Also, Ed has given you a new phone number for one of the customers, and he wants you to change the number for the billing statement.

1. Sort the mail merge recipients in ascending order by last name.

2. Edit the entry for Allen Banks and change his phone number to **215 828-1235**.

H. Create Mailing Labels

To allow Ed to mail the billing statements, you create mailing labels using the customer database as the source for the address information. Format the labels so that you can print them using the store's available label paper. The store has Avery label paper, product number 5160.

1. Create a new document and save it as **labels.doc**.

2. Create mailing labels formatted for Avery label paper, product 5160.

3. Use **Customers.txt** as the source for the mail merge recipients. The labels should be in alphabetical order by the last names of the customers.

4. Format the labels as an address block. If necessary, match the mail merge field names with the database field names.

I. Create Envelopes

Ed is considering the option of printing envelopes with each customer's name and address information instead of printing labels. He has recently purchased a new printer and would like to test this feature. As a result, he has asked you to create standard size 10 envelopes for the billing statements.

1. Create a new document and save it as **envelopes.doc**.

2. Use the Mail Merge Wizard to create envelopes, formatted for the standard size 10 envelopes.

3. Use **Customers.txt** as the source for the mail merge recipients. The labels should be in alphabetical order by the last names of the customers. Use the store name and address for the return address on the envelopes.

PROJECT RESULTS |

Upon completion of the project, you should have the following files:
>   **billing.doc**
>   **labels.doc**
>   **envelopes.doc**

HIGH SCHOOL DRAMA CLASS

PROBLEM STATEMENT

You have just learned that you will be teaching the high school drama class next semester, and you have decided to prepare in advance some of the documents you'll need for this class. The first document you need to create is the course syllabus. The syllabus contains all the information about the course including the course objectives, grading criteria, and course policies.

The Junior/Senior drama class traditionally takes a three-day field trip to New York so that students can attend two Broadway plays. Some of the teachers have suggested that you send a letter to the student's parents early in the semester, to inform them of the upcoming trip. You are also interested in capturing student evaluations of the trip, which will be valuable as you plan for future trips. You want to be able to post the evaluation form online for students' easy access.

AVAILABLE DATA

Data files: **parents.mdb; Drama Objectives.doc; Standard Syllabus.doc, Letter Body.doc**

The list of parents has been prepared for you by the office staff. The list is created as a standard Mail Merge Source file (.mdb).

The Drama Objectives document contains the objectives that have been specified for this course by the Drama department chairman. You also need to include the standard syllabus content required by the school. The Letter Body document forms the body of the letter to parents. You need to merge this letter with the parents' data.

TASKS

A. Create the Syllabus

In constructing your syllabus, you need to include the information supplied by the drama department and the school's standard syllabus content.

1. Enter the data shown in Figure 1 and then save it as **Drama Syllabus.doc**. Although you will want to use a table for alignment purposes, you don't want your syllabus to look like a table.

FIGURE 1   Drama Syllabus

Instructor:	Your name
Office:	Room 115
Office Hours:	MWF 3:00–4:00 p.m. TH 3:30–4:30 p.m.
Phone:	Your phone number
E-mail:	Your e-mail address
Web site:	http://www.HighSchool.edu/~YourName
Text:	*Drama for High School Students*, Steven Brinkley, Ed.D., 3rd ed., Prentice Press, Inc., 1999. ISBN: 0764599084
	Acting as a Career, Cheri Milton and Eugene Scott, Franklin Publishing Co., 2000. ISBN: 8976-908
Supplies:	Notebook, pen, and pencil
Prerequisites:	English composition Freshman Drama
Grading:	Participation/Discussion 15%
	Research Projects: 10%
	Dramatic Presentations: 30%
	Tests: 45%
Grading Scale:	95–100=A, 85–94=B, 75–84=C, 65–74=D, 0–64=F

2. On the line above the table, center and bold the title **Junior/Senior Drama Course**. Insert the date of the upcoming semester on the line below the title.

3. Insert the file **Standard Syllabus.doc** below the table.

4. Insert the file **Drama Objectives.doc** below the standard syllabus.

B. Format the Course Title

You would like the syllabus to be attractive and inspire your students. Looking ahead, you realize you would probably want the same title and graphic on all your materials for this course. You decide to use a macro to create the title. Refer to Figure 2, in Task G, for a sample title, but yours does not have to follow this example exactly.

1. Delete the existing title on the syllabus.

2. Begin recording a new macro named **DramaTitle** which is available to all other documents (attach the macro to the Normal template). The macro should run by pressing **Ctrl+T**.

3. While the Macro recorder is running, use WordArt to create the title. Choose whatever style you think would look best. Center the WordArt at the top of the document and insert a drama-related clip art underneath. When finished, stop the Macro Recorder.

4. Delete the title you just created and run your macro to verify that it works correctly.

5. Using the VB editor, add your name and the date in the comments of the macro.

C. Create the Field Trip Form Letter

You want to inform your students' parents early on in the semester that there will be a field trip, although you don't have the specific details at this time. Since the parents' names and addresses have already been provided to you in a Mail Merge source file (.mdb), you need to prepare the letter to be merged with the parents' information.

1. Open the file **Letter Body.doc** in Word and save it as **Parent Letter.doc**

2. Run the macro you created in the previous task so the title appears on the top of this document.

3. Start the Mail Merge Wizard, and specify Letter as the document type using the current document. Use the **parents.mdf** file as the recipients list.

4. Insert the following fields into the letter:
   - *Date* field at the top of the letter
   - *Title*, *First_Name*, and *Last_Name* on the same line
   - *Address_Line_1*
   - *City*, *State*, and *ZIP_code* fields
   - Insert a salutation followed by the *Title* and *LastName* fields
   - Replace "your child" with the *Child* field in the first sentence of the first paragraph
   - Replace "Student Name" with your name and "Fictitious Phone Number" with your phone number.

D. Edit the Parent List

The office wants to include your letters with their other bulk mailings, so you need to sort the list by zip code. Since you're looking at the list, you also quickly proofread it.

1. You notice that there are two entries for John Smith at the same address. You don't need to send two letters, so you delete one of those entries.

2. Sort the parents file in ascending order by zip code.

E. Merge the Form Letter with the Parents Information

Now that the letter has been prepared and the parent list is as you want it, you are ready to merge the form letter with the parents' list.

1. Preview the letter to make sure the field codes are in their proper position, and merge the letters. Save the merged document as **Parent Letter Merged.doc**. Print the first three letters only.

F. Create Mailing Labels

You are using school envelopes that already have the return address printed on them, so you just need to create mailing labels for the envelopes.

1. Create a new document named **Parent Labels.doc**.

2. Format the labels for Avery labels #5160.

3. Use the **parents.mdb** (the same file you used when you merged the letters) to create a mailing label for each parent. Save the merged labels as **Parent Labels.doc**.

G. Request a Trip Evaluation

You already know you will want the students to evaluate their trip when they return, as it will help in planning next year's trip. Your network administrator has explained that if you create an onscreen form, he can place it on the network. Students can then log into their accounts and fill out the form.

1. Create a new document titled **Evaluation.doc**, and use the macro you created earlier to place the heading on the top of the form.

2. Below the title, create a form that resembles Figure 2. Make sure to include the following requirements:

   - Note that students will be able to select two plays to attend from a choice of four: *Cats*; *My Fair Lady*; *Kiss Me Kate*; and *The Tapdance Kid*.
   - On the form, include both check boxes and drop-down lists when multiple choice answers are required.
   - Several of the questions require a short answer.

3. When you have completed the form, save it as a Web page.

FIGURE 2 Field Trip Evaluation Form

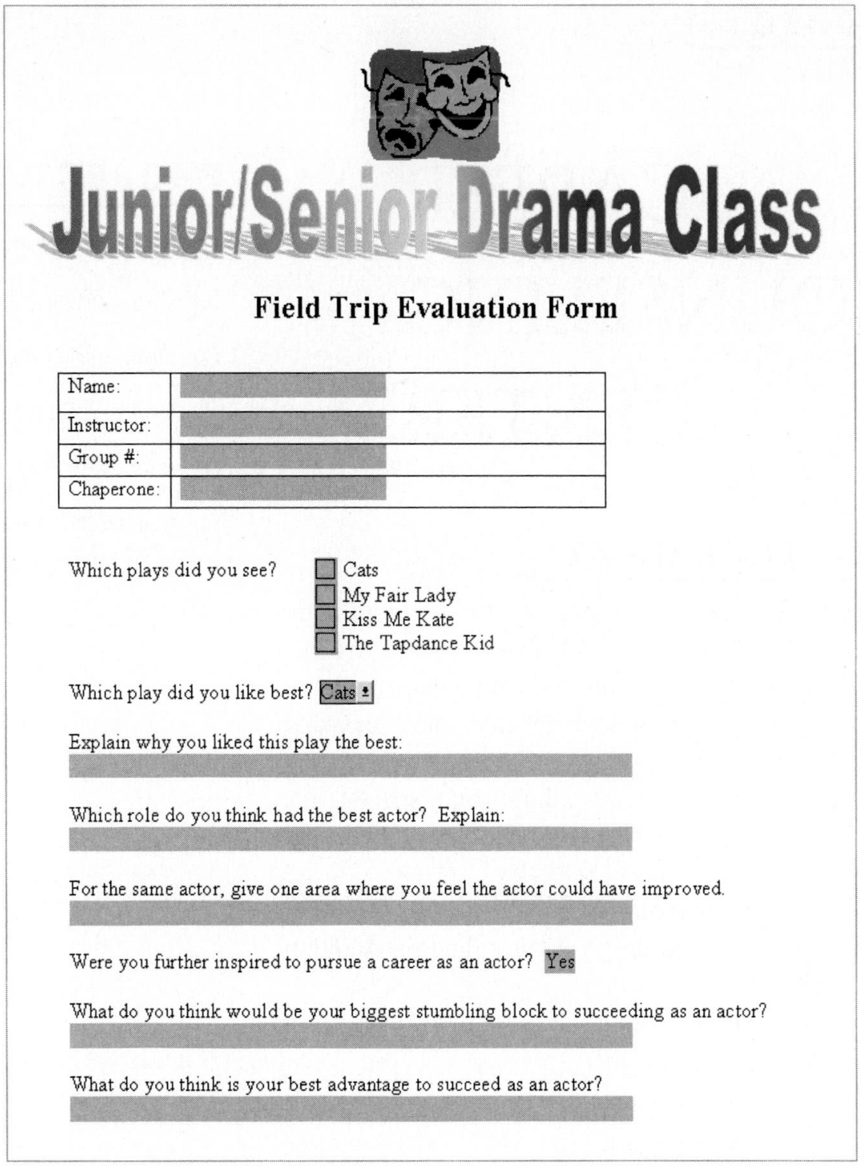

Junior/Senior Drama Class

Field Trip Evaluation Form

Name:	
Instructor:	
Group #:	
Chaperone:	

Which plays did you see?
- [ ] Cats
- [ ] My Fair Lady
- [ ] Kiss Me Kate
- [ ] The Tapdance Kid

Which play did you like best? Cats

Explain why you liked this play the best:

Which role do you think had the best actor? Explain:

For the same actor, give one area where you feel the actor could have improved.

Were you further inspired to pursue a career as an actor? Yes

What do you think would be your biggest stumbling block to succeeding as an actor?

What do you think is your best advantage to succeed as an actor?

PROJECT RESULTS

Upon completion of this project, you should have the following documents:

Drama Syllabus.doc
Evaluation.doc
Evaluation.htm
Evaluation_files folder
Parent Letter.doc
Parent Letter Merged.doc
Parent Labels.doc

CAREER COUNSELING CENTER

PROBLEM STATEMENT

You have been asked by the director of the Career Counseling Center (CCC) of your university to develop a sample Excel spreadsheet that will assist accounting graduates to consider various aspects of what it takes to make an informed job placement decision. After speaking with a number of accounting professors, you have determined that some of the "hot" job markets are Los Angeles, Chicago, and Atlanta; however, you are to find information for one other location (of your own choosing) as well.

To assist a variety of students, you have decided to include a number of accounting related positions: Accountant, Auditor (Internal Auditing is in demand), and Loan Analyst.

The CCC director wants you to take into account a wide variety of data when evaluating potential job markets:

■ Salary for each job type for each city

■ Cost of living factors for each of these cities

■ Quality of life factors, such as crime index and education expenditures

AVAILABLE DATA

Data Files: **CCCAccounting.xls**

Be sure to enter your name and date (use a date function) in the Documentation sheet. Save the workbook as **CCCAccounting2.xls** or following the naming directions provided by your instructor.

Web Sites: For relevant Web sites, visit the Student Online Companion at **www.course.com/downloads/sites/projects**.

TASKS |

A. Statistical Research

A number of Web sites exist that provide information about salaries as well as cost of living and quality of life. This task involves searching for appropriate data on the Web. In most cases the data you need will be in the necessary format, but in other instances you may have to manipulate the data in the worksheet. Refer to more than one Web site to obtain the data needed for this case.

1. Conduct an Internet search of four cities (Los Angeles, Chicago, Atlanta, and a city of your choice) to locate the necessary statistical data, as outlined below. Use the Student Online Companion as a starting point. Enter your findings into the appropriate cells of the **Job Data** worksheet in the **CCCAccounting2.xls** workbook.

Salary Data

Capture the high and low salaries for each city for the following positions (assume entry level for all):

- Accountant
- Auditor
- Loan Analyst (often found under Banking)

Quality of Life Factors

Capture the statistics listed in Figure 1 for each city: Los Angeles, Chicago, Atlanta, and a city of your own choosing. Some of the factors regarding quality of life are expressed as index numbers. Index numbers are based on a national average of 100. Your city's number will be higher or lower, but will usually be expressed as a 3-digit value. Using an index number allows you to compare factors between cities.

FIGURE 1   Quality-of-life Factors

Factor	Method of Measurement
Crime rate	Use an index number, not dollars, for crimes; crime rates are also expressed as number of crimes per 100,000 population
Per pupil spending	Use the state's most recent reported per pupil expenditure
Utility index	Use an index number, not dollars, for utilities; another method would be to use percentages; in this case it represents a percentage of income this item consumes
Food index	Use an index number, not dollars, for groceries; as with the utility index, another method is to use percentages
Housing prices	Assume a 2000 square foot house (approximately) for real estate pricing
Property taxes	Use percent of property value, but note that you may need to do your own calculations to determine these percentages
Income taxes	Use percent of income, but note that you may need to do your own calculations to determine these percentages

2. Format the **Job Data** worksheet for a professional appearance. This may include changing cell background colors as needed to enhance readability of data columns and rows. Make sure cell widths are adjusted to allow all data and text to be read.

B. City Comparisons

Now that you have researched and entered the raw data for each city, you use this data to compare the cities to allow the accounting graduate to make an employment decision based on factors other than salary alone.

1. Using the data for all the cities, calculate a "geographical" average, minimum, and maximum for each factor. For the salary data, calculate the average, minimum, and maximum for both the high- and low-salary figures.

2. Use formulas to show how each city compares favorably or unfavorably to the geographical averages. (Use a difference calculation that involves the city average against the geographical group average.)

3. Look carefully at all the salary data and comparisons you have created. Based on your data, choose one job that you would recommend to an accounting graduate. Name the cell for the selected job **Job** and create a 3-D cell reference from Job to the Recommended Job cell in the **Documentation** worksheet so that the chosen job's name is displayed. (Use the cell name, not its reference.)

4. Based on your recommended job, create a column chart of the high and low salaries for all four cities as a new worksheet labeled **Salary Chart**. Add appropriate labels and legend.

5. Format the chart to be professional in appearance. Use an appropriate monetary-type graphic (from clip art) rather than a color as the column fill effect (use the stack, not stretch, effect).

6. Create seven additional charts (each on a separate worksheet) that compare each of the life factors for the four cities you are comparing. Recommended chart types include column, bar, line, cylinder, cone, and pyramid. Use of chart subtypes is encouraged. Remember that some chart types have specific uses and are not appropriate (e.g. data used in pie charts must equal 100%).

   Quality-of-life factors: Crime Rate, Per Pupil Spending, Utility Index, Food Index, Housing Price, Property Taxes, Income Taxes

7. Format each of the charts in a professional manner and add appropriate labels.

8. Return to the **Job Data** worksheet and calculate the average salary for the job you recommended, based upon the high and low salaries you found, for all four cities.

9. Carefully consider the average salaries as well as the nonsalary factors for each city. Based upon the job you recommended, select the city that you would recommend. Create two 3-D cell references from the **Job Data** worksheet to the **Documentation** worksheet using cell names, not cell references (you need to name the cells prior to creating the 3-D cell references). The first should be from the City's label cell to the Recommended City cell, and the second, from the city's Average Salary cell to the Average Salary cell in the **Documentation** worksheet.

10. Format the Average Salary cell for your selected city on the **Job Data** worksheet so that it is different from all the others (include a cell comment that is constantly visible, indicating that this is your recommendation).

C. Determine Housing Costs

Graduates need to consider housing costs when making their employment decisions. Prepare a mortgage amortization table using the **Mortgage** worksheet showing the costs to buy the average priced home in the recommended city.

1. Calculate two principal and interest payments, one based on a 30-year mortgage and the second based on a 15-year mortgage. Find current interest rates for 30-year and 15-year terms on the Internet or in a financial publication. Base the mortgage payments on the average house price for the city you've selected (use 3-D cell references to the Job Data worksheet).

2. Calculate the monthly house insurance costs based on the house price multiplied by $3.50 per thousand of value divided by 12.

3. Calculate your monthly home taxes based upon the property tax rate divided by 12, times the value of your home.

4. Calculate the gross monthly payment (principal and interest plus insurance plus property taxes). Do not complete the full amortization table at this time. You will return to complete it during the next task.

5. When done, format the worksheet, including the data labels, to be professional in appearance and fully legible.

D. Create a Sample Budget

Prepare a sample budget worksheet (labeled **Income Statement**) that illustrates for the accounting graduate the income and expenditures for the recommended job and city. It should include the items listed in Figure 2.

FIGURE 2   Sample Budget Items

Budget Item	Method of Calculation
Annual income	Use a 3-D cell reference from the Job Data worksheet; make sure to use the cell name, not its reference
Gross monthly income	This calculates the monthly income based on the annual average income
Federal tax (monthly)	Based on the average salary for the recommended job in the recommended city (*Hint:* Build a formula using 3-D references to use the federal tax rate from the Job Data worksheet.)
State tax (monthly)	Based on average salary (*Hint:* Build a formula using 3-D references to use the state income tax rate from the Job Data worksheet.)
Net monthly income	Monthly gross income minus taxes
Mortgage payment	Use a 3-D reference from the gross monthly payment cell in the Mortgage worksheet; make sure to choose the term that qualifies the buyer for the loan

1. Create an IF function in the cell to the right of the Mortgage Payment cell to test whether the house payment is less than or equal to 25% of net monthly income. The test should indicate if the mortgage payment would qualify or be rejected.

2. If the 15- or 30-year mortgage payment is rejected based on the average house price for the recommended city, begin reducing the loan amount in $10,000 increments on the **Mortgage** worksheet until the resulting gross monthly payment does qualify. Use this qualifying loan amount when searching for your house in the next task. If the loan amount must be changed from the city's average, indicate the change by adding a cell comment to the Loan Amount cell on the **Amortization** worksheet saying that the loan amount had to be changed and by how much.

3. Format all data and labels to be legible and professional in appearance.

4. Return to the **Mortgage** worksheet, and build a complete amortization table based on the loan that you can qualify to receive. Use a payment starting date of July 1, 2005.

E. Search for a Home

1. Conduct an Internet search to locate real estate listings for the recommended city. You will find real estate links on the Student Online Companion.

2. Find a Web page that shows a picture (if possible), along with a description and price for a home at or slightly below the average price for that city, or that qualifies to receive financing.

3. Create a hyperlink in the **Documentation** worksheet to the real estate Web page of the house located in the previous step, and provide a short description and/or address for the property in the Description cell (this is particularly important if the hyperlink leads to a general listing of many homes). Be sure the text that appears in the cell is descriptive of, not the same as, the actual URL.

F. Finalize the Worksheet

1. Save the workbook as a noninteractive Web page. It should have an appropriate title and a file name of **CCCAccounting2.htm**.

2. When all work is complete and you are satisfied that the data is correct, protect all worksheets in the workbook. Do not set a password.

PROJECT RESULTS |

Your completed project should include the following files and folders:

CCCAccounting2.xls

CCCAccounting2.htm

CCCAccounting2_Files folder

LES BEAUX CLOTHIERS

PROBLEM STATEMENT

Les Beaux is a designer clothing manufacturer interested in improving service to their retailers, as well as improving their financial tracking of the various profit components. The firm has a huge database that stores all the data associated with its retailers, clothing, and billing. To improve service, the management has hired you to thoroughly examine the retailer and clothing information for a sample month's orders.

Your job is to analyze the data and report back to management. You need to determine what tools and functions are most appropriate for each task. Remember that all calculations should be based on input values that can be easily modified (i.e., price of an item is in only one place and all calculations requiring price refer back to that original input cell). Additionally, your final spreadsheet should look professional. This may require modifying the format, text wrapping, fonts, colors, and so on, as you see fit.

AVAILABLE DATA

Data Files: **lesbeaux.xls**

The **lesbeaux.xls** workbook contains two worksheets (**Items** and **Orders**), which are detailed in Figures 1 and 2.

FIGURE 1   Items Worksheet

Entry	Description
Item#	Unique identification code
Description	Description of clothing item
Selling price	Price charged to retailers for each clothing item
Materials cost	Cost of fabric, trimmings, etc. required for manufacturing
Lead time	Average delivery time for item

FIGURE 2   Orders Worksheet

Entry	Description
Order#	Unique order identification number
Account#	Retailer number that placed this order (Information about the specific retailers is not available on the spreadsheet at this time. Retailers are often large, multiple-store organizations that order quantities to be used at their multiple locations.)
Quantity	Number of items ordered
Item#	Type of item ordered
Date ordered	Day the retailer placed the order
Date delivered	Day the retailer received the item

TASKS

A. Profit Calculations and Analysis

In this section you will be calculating the revenues, various expenses, and profit per item and per order. Once you have determined these values, you will be aggregating the values and summarizing profits into groupings which will help Les Beaux ultimately make decisions about their various customers and various items that are sold.

1. Expand the **Orders** worksheet to include the data in the following columns. Split the windows so that the **Order#** and **Category** headings always appear on the sheet, making the worksheet easier to manipulate. A definition of each field is listed below.

All formulas should be written so that you can copy the formulas down the column without the need for modification. Add these columns in the order shown.

- **Selling Price per Item** is the value listed on the Items worksheet. Reference the selling price for the correct corresponding item.

- **Material Costs per Item** is the value listed on the Items worksheet. Again, reference the items worksheet for the correct corresponding item.

- **Shipping Costs per Item** are calculated as $2.50 or 5% of the material costs, whichever is greater. Record the $2.50 minimum charge and the percentage into a cell on a separate part of the **Orders** worksheet named **Inputs**, so they can later be used to create a what-if scenario.

- **Labor Costs per Item** are estimated as a function of the material costs and can be calculated as follows. Record any necessary values in the inputs section you set up in the previous step.
  - Labor costs for items with material costs of less than $100 are estimated at 100% of material costs.
  - Labor costs for items with material costs of at least $100 but less than $500 are estimated at 50% of material costs.
  - Labor costs for items with material costs of at least $500 are estimated at 20% of material costs.

- **Overhead Costs** are $100,000 per month. Save this value as the range name **Overhead**. For ease, this total overhead is applied equally to each item sold regardless of price. So, if a total of 25,000 items were sold in the month (total for all orders), each individual item would be 1/25,000 of the overhead expense. Round this value to the nearest cent.

- **Profit per Item** is revenue per item minus total expenses per item.

- **Total Revenues per Order** is the selling price per item multiplied by the number of items. Similarly, all the other expense breakdowns per order are also the expense per item times the number of items. Write a single formula and copy this both down and across to fill in the columns for **Total Revenues, Total Material Costs, Total Shipping, Total Labor, Total Overhead,** and **Total Profit per Order**. Display the values in currency format with no decimal places.

- **Profit Margin** is the percentage of profit to revenue. Format this information as a percentage and round this calculation to the nearest tenth of a percent.

2. Perform the following aggregate calculations at the bottom of the table you have created. Skip a least one line after the order data and highlight the blank line with yellow.

   - Calculate averages for each item starting with the Selling Price and copying it across all the way to profit.

   - Calculate the total revenues for the month, and copy the formula across to fill in the totals for each expense item.

   - Calculate the average profit margin based on the aggregate revenue and profit values.

3. Analyze the orders by profit margin category. In a separate column adjacent to the orders list, write a formula to determine the profit margin category of each item. Label this column **Profit Category**. The formulas should be written so the resulting value and formatting are automatically updated if there are changes to the input values.

   - Display the word **High** in the color blue (bolded) for all orders with profit margins over 40%.

   - Display the word **Low** in the color black (bolded) for all orders with profit margins between 0% and 40% inclusive.

   - Display the word **Loss** in the color red (bolded) for all that lost money.

4. On a separate worksheet, create a table that summarizes the profit margin categories you just created. Include the total number of orders and total profits from orders for each category. Label this worksheet **Category**. Make sure the formulas you use are automatically updated if any of the order values change.

5. On a new worksheet, create a PivotTable that shows, by item and by customer account, the total revenues and total profits of all orders for this month. Use **Account#** for the columns and **Item#** for the rows. Label this worksheet **Profit**.

6. Copy the row containing profit by customer account to just below the PivotTable. Calculate the percent of total profit earned from that company. Total profit earned from a customer is determined by dividing the customer's profit by Les Beaux's total profit.

B. Analyze Service to Customers

In addition to being concerned about profits, management is also concerned with service to their customers. The most critical service concern is "on-time delivery." Customers are given lead time in the number of days from order placement to delivery. Additionally, Les Beaux has asked you to estimate the cost to the company if it were to retroactively give a 10% rebate (based on total sales price) on each late order.

1. Create a column on the Orders worksheet to determine for each order if it was on time. Remember, lead times are given in days and are listed by item number on the Items table. Make sure to write a formula that can be copied down the column.

   - **On Time** is indicated by a True value (delivered on or before the date it should have arrived).
   - **Late** is indicated by a False value (delivery arrived after the expected arrival date).

2. Les Beaux has asked you to estimate the cost to the company if it were to retroactively give a 10% rebate (based on total sales price) on each order that was late. Add another column to the Orders worksheet to calculate the rebate value by order (zero dollars if no rebate) and the total for all orders.

3. Create another PivotTable to determine by customer the number of orders that were on time and the number of orders that were not on time. Label this worksheet **Delivery**.

C. Explore Alternate Scenarios

1. The shipping service Les Beaux uses is discussing a rate increase and has presented alternative pricing schemes. You need to determine the effect these changes have on shipping costs and overall profits. Once you have explored the impact of the different scenarios, include in your recommendation which pricing scheme is most advantageous for Les Beaux.

   To perform these analyses use the Scenarios tool. Save the original values as **Original**, then save each subsequent scenario as **Scenario1**, **Scenario2**, and so forth. After inputting each scenario, create a worksheet labeled **Scenario Summary**.

   Option 1: The shipping costs percentage is raised to 8% from 5%, and the minimum charge increases from $2.50 to $5.00.

   Option 2: The shipping costs are raised to 6% from 5%, and the minimum charge increases from $2.50 to $15.

   Option 3: The shipping costs percentage is raised to 10% with no minimum charge.

2. Determine an alternate item price for Black Skirts (item #8) that would generate a total overall profit of an additional $100,000 over existing profits. Without altering the current price for the item, record this new price on the **Scenario Summary** worksheet.

   Is this a reasonable price for a skirt? Compare your results with at least three other retailers and include your recommendation on the Scenario Summary sheet. To determine reasonable prices for a good quality black skirt, search the Internet for similar designer skirts. Reference at least three different Web sites. Note the Internet addresses where you found your data on the **Scenario Summary** worksheet.

D. Profitability Analysis Summary and Recommendations

At this point, you have enough data to make some recommendations to the company regarding which items may require further investigation into pricing or whether or not the company should sell a particular item at all. You may also have recommendations on which customers should be given preferential treatment based on the total amount of business that is conducted with them.

Item Recommendations

1. On the **Items** worksheet add a column to summarize the total profits by item. (One possible method is to use the SUMIF function.)

2. Create a second new column on the **Items** worksheet offering the following recommendations by item:
   - **Discontinue** if the profit for the item is negative (i.e., the company is losing money).
   - **Continue** *As Is* if the item profit is less than 10% of the overall profit for all items, but is not losing money.
   - **Advertise** if the item profit is greater than 10% of overall profits.

3. Below the table, write out a formula to automatically determine the total number of items in each recommendation category.

Customer (Account #) Recommendations

1. Transfer the account, revenue, and profit information from the Orders worksheet into a new worksheet named **Customers**. This new worksheet should automatically be updated if any of the values on **Orders** is updated.

2. Use the Data Subtotal tools to summarize the revenues and profits for each account. When the subtotals appear, click on outline symbol **2** to show only subtotals by account.

3. Highlight the accounts that are responsible for at least 10% of overall profits.

E. Analyze New Line Launch

Management would like to launch a new designer line that will cost $8 million dollars. It is considering using a 10-year bank loan at 8% annual interest compounded quarterly. Les Beaux would make a down payment of 1% of this year's profits.

1. To estimate yearly profits, use the original one-month profit as calculated in the original scenario and assume that value for all months. What is the payment required per quarter on this loan? Include your results on the **Scenario Summary** worksheet.

F. Create a Chart for Management

As part of your presentation to management, you want to include a chart that compares the profit contributions (percent of total profit) from each of the items Les Beaux sells.

1. Prepare an easy-to-read chart that clearly illustrates this information. The legend should contain the item descriptions. Make sure to include a chart title and display the profit values. Label this new worksheet **Chart**.

PROJECT RESULTS |

Your completed **lesbeaux.xls** file should contain the following worksheets:
Items, Orders, Category, Profit, Delivery, Scenario Summary, Customers, Chart

JACKSON CATTLE

PROJECT OUTLINE

A. Annual Feed Costs

B. Capital Investment

C. Veterinary Expenses

D. Proposed Income Statement

E. Data Comparisons

F. Chart Cattle Expenses

G. Shipping Calculator

PROBLEM STATEMENT

Your friend Cal Jackson has decided to go into the cattle business. He plans to buy calves and raise them for sale. Nearby cattle-breeding operations can provide a good supply of calves at less than the market rates. Before beginning this venture, Cal would like you to help him explore the financial viability of this business by considering the revenues, expenses, and expected yearly income this business will generate. He'd like you to also compare these profits with available data from similar ventures.

In the Available Data section, Cal has summarized much of the data he gathered. Part of this data is already recorded in his worksheet **Bovine.xls**. Since you have already planned how best to organize your workbook, you are now ready to read over the available data and determine the financial viability of this business for Cal.

AVAILABLE DATA

Data files: **Bovine.xls; Bovine.txt**

Cal has collected a lot of information on cattle feeding, housing, and health needs. You will use this data in later sections to calculate specific values.

All costs should be based on a herd size of 300 head of cattle. On average it is expected that each year 2/3 of the total herd will mature and be sold. This cattle will be replaced by purchasing an equal number of calves.

Cattle Pricing

Assume that Cal will be buying the calves at the age of six months at the average weight of 400 pounds and selling the cattle at the age of 24 months and an average weight of 1400 pounds. Current purchase prices for calves are $0.74 per pound. The selling price this past year for mature heifers and steers was $75 per hundred pounds.

The cost of shipping of cattle to a stock yard is the responsibility of the seller. Cal was unable to find information on the costs of shipping cattle, so for the time being you are estimating the cost to be 1% of the selling price.

Feed Requirements Pricing

Based on the research Cal has done, he has decided to feed the cattle the diet outlined below. This diet varies based on the age of the cattle. The percent of the herd you expect to be in each age category is also included (estimated on this business being at a steady state). Current feed prices: corn is selling for $65 per ton (there are 2000 pounds in a ton); hay for $2.00 per bushel (there are 33.6 bushels per ton); and soy for $0.07 per pound.

FIGURE 1   Feed Requirements

Age Category	Age as % of Herd	Average Pounds of Animal	Required Dry Matter of Feed per Day as % of Body Weight	Corn as % of Diet	Hay as % of Diet	Soy as % of Diet
6–12 months	33%	600	3%	70%	25%	5%
13–23 months	61%	900	2%	85%	13%	2%
24 months	6%	1150	2%	85%	15%	0%

To calculate daily feed quantities you need to assume an average moisture content of the feed. Based on your readings, you assume that there is a 13% water component to all of the feed products you will be purchasing. So for example:

A steer in the 6–12 month category weighing an average of 600 pounds would eat 18 pounds (3% times 600 pounds) of dry matter. Including moisture content this equals 18/(100%–13%) which is 20.69 pounds of food per day. Of this 20.69 pounds, 14.48 pounds is corn (70% of 20.69).

Thus, the daily cost of the corn for one steer in this age category is 14.48 pounds per day multiplied by $65 dollars per ton of corn divided by 2000 lbs per ton.

Barn Pricing

Cal has called the Ohio Agricultural Extension program at Ohio State University to get some advice on facilities requirements for raising cattle. He has learned that normally barns are provided with adjacent lots, so the cattle can move from inside to outside. Based on this information, Cal has decided to allow 20 square feet per animal in the barn and 50 square feet of paved lot.

Cal has also contacted local contractors for information regarding construction costs of the barn, paving of the lot, and perimeter fencing. He was quoted $25 per square foot of barn area, which includes the construction of lofts, utilities, and so on. Paving costs are $3.00 per square yard (9 square feet/square yard). The cost of fencing runs $25 per linear foot of fence.

Veterinary Expenses

In addition to feeding and housing the animals, there are other expenses necessary to maintain optimal health of the animals. Cal will need to make some decisions regarding which immunizations and vitamins they receive, in addition to accounting for normal outbreaks of diseases.

There are several preventative and nutritional treatments being considered. Figure 2 contains a list of each treatment and the recommended season(s) it is given, as noted by a True value. Included is the expected cost per head and the expected percentage of head that will need it in the seasons listed. For example, the cost of antibiotic treatment is the total number of head times 10% of the herd times four per year times the $0.35 per treatment. In addition to the cost of the treatments, some require veterinary supervision. (Veterinary supervision costs are detailed in Task C).

FIGURE 2   Veterinary Treatments

Treatment	Winter	Spring	Summer	Autumn	Cost per Animal per Treatment	% Herd Requiring Treatment
Antibiotics	True	True	True	True	.35	10%
5-1 Vaccine	False	True	False	False	.23	100%
Nutritional Supplements	True	True	False	True	.02	100%
Mange/Lice	True	False	False	False	.35	15%

TASKS

A. Annual Feed Costs

1. Open the worksheet **Bovine.xls** and modify the formatting as follows:

   - Name the Feed requirements sheet **Feed** and change the tab color to yellow.
   - Add a row at the top of the sheet and center a title over the diet percentages labeled **Diet Components**.
   - Adjust the column widths and wrap text so that the titles appear in a similar format to the table in Figure 1.
   - Use percent formatting for all cells displaying a percentage.
   - Highlight the different sections as you proceed through this project to make it easier to locate and read the information you generate.

2. Create a second worksheet in the workbook to list the feed prices in dollars per unit (tons, bushels, etc.), and then calculate their associated cost per pound.

FIGURE 3   Feed Prices

	Corn	Hay	Soy
Price	$65.00	$2.00	$0.07
Unit	ton	bushel	pound
Price/lb	?	?	?

On the same worksheet, also include a table of additional values that are needed in your calculations such as number of head of cattle, and number of days per year (365), the percent moisture of feed, pounds per ton, and so on.

These values should all be explicitly listed in case your assumptions change later. Give range names to these pieces of data so they can easily be used in later calculations. Name the worksheet **Data** and give it a blue tab. You will be using this worksheet throughout this project to record data inputs.

3. Create four new columns on the **Feed** worksheet to list pounds per day of each of the three diet components (i.e., pounds per day of corn, hay, soy) and a total feed per day for all types. At the top, center the title, **Pounds per Animal per Day**, over these four columns.

4. Calculate the number of pounds per day per animal of corn for the 6–12 month category and copy it down into the other two age categories and across to calculate pounds of hay and soy. Write your formula with the correct cell referencing so that only one formula is needed. Remember all values should be referenced to input cells to facilitate modifications later on. Display your values with two decimal places.

   - In the Pounds per Animal per Day *Total* column, calculate the total pounds of feed per day for each age category.
   - Create a new row named **Subtotals**, just below the age categories. In that row, calculate the total pounds of feed per day for each type of feed.

5. Create another set of four columns on the **Feed** worksheet to list the total costs of feed per year for each specific feed and a total for all feed types. Center the title, **Dollars per Year**, over these calculations.

6. Calculate the total costs of feed per year for all cattle in the 6–12 month age category for corn, and copy it down into the other two categories and across to calculate these totals for hay and soy. Write your formulas with the correct cell referencing so that only one formula is needed. Format all of the cost-related columns as currency, and round the values to the nearest dollar. (*Hint*: Use the ROUND function.)

   - In the *Total* column, calculate total cost per year for each age category.
   - In the *Subtotals* row, calculate the total cost per year by feed type.

B. Capital Investment

Cal is not only concerned about the cost of feeding the cattle. He also needs to build a barn and adjacent lot areas to house the cattle. First determine the size of these facilities and then explore several financing options for Cal. In addition, you need to calculate the depreciation of these proposed facilities, so Cal can reduce his tax liability (taxes owed).

1. Using a new worksheet named **Barn** (green tab), calculate the following capital costs based on the information that was previously gathered. Make sure to explicitly list all input values and conversion factors.

   - Cost of the barn
   - Cost of the pen area
   - Cost of the fencing (assume the fencing is around all sides of the pen area, which will be constructed in a square layout)
   - Summarize the total cost of the new facility.

2. Using the **Barn** worksheet, compare three different financing options. For each option determine the present value, future value, payment per month, duration in number of

years, the number of periods per year, and the annual interest rate. Highlight any values that you calculate.

> *Option 1*: The contractor Cal is planning to use has offered Cal financing. He has told Cal he will build this facility for the price just estimated. His terms are for payments of $3,220 per month, payable over the next five years.

> *Option 2*: The bank is also willing to loan Cal the total value of the building for 5½% annual interest rate compounded monthly, with a final balloon payment of $10,000. The loan is payable monthly over the next 10 years.

> *Option 3*: Cal's third option is to see if he can generate sufficient funds by cashing in some municipal bonds he inherited. These bonds mature next month. The bonds are zero coupon (no interest payments are made until maturity) and were originally purchased for $65,000. They have been earning 6% interest compounded quarterly for the last 15 years.

Optimally Cal would like to use this inheritance to finance these facilities, but only if the bonds yield sufficient funds to pay for the full cost of the facilities. Otherwise, you recommend Cal choose the option with the lowest interest rate. Write a formula just below your analysis to automatically determine which option you are recommending to Cal.

3. In addition to considering the monthly outlay that is required to service the debt on the new barn, Cal also needs to know the annual depreciation that he is allowed to use to reduce his tax liability.

Using the straight-line depreciation method and the assumption that the facilities have a usable life of 10 years with no salvage value, write a formula to calculate the annual amount allowed for depreciation. Include the formula on the **Barn** worksheet. Again make sure all input values are explicitly listed on this worksheet.

C. Veterinary Expenses

1. Create a new worksheet titled **Vet** (color tab red). Input the Veterinary Treatments table provided in the data section. Make sure to input the Boolean values True and False as values and not as text.

2. In a column adjacent to the veterinary treatments data, calculate the yearly cost of each treatment. Write the formula for the antibiotics such that it can be copied down to calculate the cost of the other four treatments. Make sure that any input values you use are explicitly listed on the **Vet** worksheet.

3. In a row just below the data, write a formula to determine (True/False) if only antibiotics need to be administered during the winter season. Copy the formula across the row to determine this for all other seasons. (*Hint*: You do not need to use an IF function. Instead, use a combination of Boolean functions And, Or, Not.)

4. In the next row, write a formula to determine (True/False) if antibiotics and one or both of the nutritional supplements and/or Mange/Lice treatment needs to be administered in winter. Copy the formula across the row to determine this for all other seasons.

5. In the following row, write a formula to calculate the total costs of veterinary visits during winter. Copy the formula across the row to determine this for all other seasons. The criteria to use are as follows. Add this information to the **Data** worksheet.

- If the 5-1 vaccine is administered, with or without any other treatment, the veterinarian must make two visits. The charge for that is $2 per head; if the entire herd is treated (100%) then the cost is $2 times the total number of animals in the herd.

- If the vet is coming to administer only antibiotics, then the charge for that is $1 per head for only those cattle treated.

- If the vet is coming to administer antibiotics and one or both of the nutritional supplements and/or Mange/Lice treatment, the charge is $1 per head for each animal in the herd.

6. Calculate the yearly total costs for all treatments, for veterinary visits, and totals for both. Highlight these values.

D. Proposed Income Statement

Now you are ready to put together a yearly income statement for Cal.

1. Create a new worksheet named **Income.** On this worksheet, calculate the following information on a per year basis. Any additional input values should be explicitly listed on the **Data** worksheet.

- **Sales Revenues**: Amount earned from the sale of cattle during one year
- **Shipping Costs**: Cost to ship these cattle
- **New Calves**: Cost to purchase new calves to replace cattle sold
- **Cost of Feed**: Yearly cost to feed the cattle
- **Loan Payments**: For barn facilities based on your recommended option
- **Veterinary Expenses:** Include costs of treatment for all four seasons
- **Labor Expenses**: Assume 10 hours per week of help at $5 per hour (52 weeks per year)
- **Profit before taxes**: Sales revenue minus all expenses
- **Taxes**: 15% flat rate times taxable income (*Hint*: Taxable income is profit before tax less depreciation.)
- **Profit after Taxes**: Profit before taxes less tax
- **Profit per Head**: Profit after tax divided by the herd size

E. Data Comparisons

A nearby cattle breeder has collected data on the profit per head for a number of cattle operations in several different countries. She is willing to share it with you and Cal as long as you send her any additional analyses you perform with the data. Because she has a different computer system, she has sent you the data in a comma-delimited text file.

What interests you and Cal the most in the data she sent is the profit per head from U.S. firms producing category AA and AB cattle. You have decided to isolate this data to make it easier to use.

1. Import the file **bovine.txt** (comma delimited) to a new worksheet named **Comparison** (pink tab) in your workbook.

2. Split the Category Lot column into two columns, one listing the 2-letter category and the other listing the three-digit lot. Remove the original column.

3. Sort the data alphabetically by category and then by lot number, highest first.

4. Resave the data on this sheet only as a comma-delimited file, so that your friend can import it back into his system. Name the file **Calsdata.csv**.

5. Filter the data to display only category AA and AB operations that are located in the United States.

F. Chart Cattle Expenses

1. Create a chart on a new worksheet that will *best* illustrate the detail expenses involved in Cal's cattle operation. Name the worksheet **Chart**, and choose a color tab not already used.

2. Add the title **Cattle Expenses** to the chart. The x axis should read **Category** and the y axis **Dollars**. Do not include a legend. Modify the chart for a professional appearance, giving each category a different color.

G. Shipping Calculator

Cal has also asked you to look into shipping costs. Based on several phone calls, you have collected the following information:

- Costs for a full truckload of steer/heifers (30 to 50 animals) runs $2.50 per mile for the entire truckload with a minimum charge of $500.
- Costs for less than a full truckload of steer/heifers costs .06 cents per 1000 pounds per mile. Assume each steer is 1400 pounds on average. There is a minimum charge of $200 per shipment.

You decide to create a shipping calculator for Cal to make it easier for him to determine his shipping costs. To use the calculator, Cal just needs to input the number of head in a shipment and the distance in miles, and then the shipping costs are displayed with a click of a button. (*Note:* This calculator is not a VBA form; it does not require the use of input or message boxes.)

1. Open a new workbook and save it as **Shipping.xls**. Create the calculator as shown in Figure 4 using formatting techniques. Include the following constraints in your calculator:

- **Number of head to be shipped** should be a whole number between 1 and 50.
- **Number of miles to be shipped** should be at least 1.
- Set up input messages that are displayed if the entries fall outside the constraints.
- Modify the worksheet so that automatic calculation is turned off.

FIGURE 4   Shipping Calculator Design

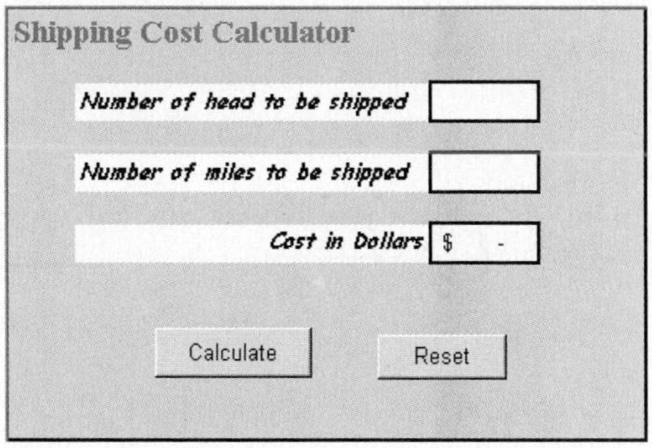

2. Create two buttons on the form that can:

- Automatically calculate the Cost in Dollars with the inputted values. Since automatic calculation is turned off, this button requires a macro.

- Automatically reset the input boxes to blank.

3. Hide the all toolbars, sheet tabs, and status bars. Unlock cells which Cal needs to input data.

4. Protect the form so that Cal can select both locked and unlocked cells, but not be able to change unlocked cells.

PROJECT RESULTS

At the completion of this project, you will have the following files:

Bovine.xls containing worksheets: **Feed**; **Data**; **Barn**; **Vet**; **Income**; **Comparison**; **Chart**

Calsdata.csv

Shipping.xls

MEDCURES, INC.

PROBLEM STATEMENT

Congratulations! You have been hired as MedCures Incorporated's newest full-time employee and have been assigned to the research team of their hottest new drug—"Zobo." The Project Zobo team is currently coordinating human test trials with three major metropolitan hospitals. Zobo is a drug that appears to have a major impact on lowering blood triglyceride levels. This new drug promises to be more effective and have fewer side effects than other drugs currently available. Your job will be to first analyze the data so that you and a team of medical professionals can ascertain if these claims are true, and then to best design the appropriate protocol before continuing the process for full FDA approval.

AVAILABLE DATA

Data Files: **hospital1.txt**; **hospital2.txt**; **hospital3.txt**; **H1data.txt**; **H2data.txt**; **H3data.txt**

Three different teaching hospitals have been conducting the trials and have sent to you comma-delimited text files with their patient data. (The numbers 1, 2, and 3 represent the different hospitals.) Although each of the three files are in a slightly different format, the files do contain the same standard information:

The data files contain the following data points:

- **Participant Information**: Patient information includes Social Security number, patient name, weight in pounds (lbs), height in inches (in), and age in years.
- **Drug Protocol Used**: The five protocols are detailed in Figure 1.

PROJECT OUTLINE

A. Importing and Combining the Data

B. Data Analysis

C. Data Analysis Tools

D. Share Your Results

E. Automate Data Acquisition

F. Prepare a Budget for Phase Two Testing

FIGURE 1   Drug Protocols

Protocol	Medication	Daily Dosage in Grams/50 Kg of Weight	Comments
A	Placebo	none	Sugar pill
B	Zobo	2	Dosage given in 1 mg increments rounded to nearest milligram based on participant weight
C	Zobo	1	Dosage given in 1 mg increments rounded to nearest milligram based on participant weight
D	Zobo	3	Dosage given in 1 mg increments rounded to nearest milligram based on participant weight
E	Zobo	2	Dosage given in 1 mg increments rounded to nearest milligram based on participant weight

- **Initial Triglyceride Levels** is the value of each patient's initial triglyceride level just prior to comencement of the trial.
- **3-month Triglyceride Levels** represents the value of each patient's triglyceride level after three months on the medication.
- **6-month Triglyceride Levels** represents the value of each patient's triglyceride level after six months on the medication.

TASKS

A. Importing and Combining the Data

1. Create a new Excel workbook named **Zobo.xls**.

2. Import the data form files **hospital1.txt**, **hospital2.txt**, and **hospital3.txt**. Each of the files are in a slightly different format, though they are all comma delimited. Organize the columns as shown in Figure 2. Column headings should be highlighted and bolded, and similar in title to those in Figure 2. This may require you to combine some fields of the raw data and/or separate out other fields, depending on the file being imported. Be sure to format the Social Security number as text so numbers that begin with zero are not lost. Name the worksheet **Data**.

FIGURE 2   Column Structure for Data Worksheet

Hospital	SSN	Name	Age	M/F	Weight (lbs)	Height (in)	Drug Protocol	Initial Triglycerides	3-mo. Triglycerides	6-mo. Triglycerides

B. Data Analysis

Now your most important task is to generate information that the medical team can use to evaluate the trial results. Before proceeding to analyze the data, you need to validate the information you have received. For example, you've noticed that two of the protocols are identical and the team leader has given you the go ahead to combine them. In order to avoid possible problems with the FDA, you have also been asked to check the data to verify that all participants meet the requirements for being included in the test group. Once the data is validated, you also need to generate dosages received. This information is not provided in the dataset, but can be calculated based on the protocols being used in the study as outlined previously. Dosages, both collectively and individually, are needed when comparing protocols and later when formulating budgets.

Modifying and Selecting Data

1. You have noticed there is actually no difference between protocols B and E. Perhaps there was an error made when assigning the protocols; however, at this point it seems reasonable to combine the two sets of data. Thus, the first thing you do before analyzing the data is to replace all protocol values of E with B's.

2. Another problem that you've noticed is that some of the data indicates that certain participants should have been ineligible to take part in the study. Eligibility required that both of the following criteria are met:

   - The participant be under the age of 80 (Name this constant **MaxAge**.)
   - The participant has a body mass index of no more than 3.5. Body mass is measured by weight in pounds divided by height in inches. (Name this constant **BM**.)

   In a column adjacent to the imported data, determine if each participant meets the qualifications (True/False). False values should be noted with red bold lettering. Move the data records for these False values to a separate worksheet named **Reject**. On the original **Data** worksheet, hide this new column.

Calculate Actual Dosage

One key piece of data that has not been recorded is the actual number of milligrams of Zobo each participant received each day. The daily number of milligrams per 50 kilograms (kg) of body weight was provided to you by the research team. There are 2.2 pounds per kilogram (lb/kg).

1. Create a reference table on a separate worksheet named **Dosage** to record the dosages values given by the team.

2. Using an adjacent column(s) on the **Data** worksheet, calculate the actual number of milligrams taken per day for each person based on their protocol group and body weight. This formula must be written so it can be copied down the column, and will automatically update if any of the weight or dosage date is later updated. The formula must also take into account the following dosage specifications:

   - For protocols B, C, and D the minimum dosage should be 1 milligram.
   - Dosages that exceed one milligram should be rounded to the nearest whole milligram.
   - Protocol A receives no Zobo.

Statistical Analysis

You are now ready to calculate some standard statistical information to help the team get a better sense of the efficacy of this new drug. Prepare the following calculations:

1. Create two new columns adjacent to the current data to calculate the percent change in triglyceride levels (1) from the original to the 3-month check, and (2) from the original value to the 6-month check. Write the formula so it can be copied both down and across into both columns. Highlight the two columns in the same color. Percent change equals (new value – original value) divided by original value.

2. Create two additional columns in the adjacent areas to calculate the actual change (delta) (1) from the original to the 3-month check, and (2) from the original to the 6-month check. Write the formula so that it can be copied both down and across into both columns. Highlight the two columns in the same color. Delta change equals new value minus original value.

3. Skipping a row below the patient data on the **Data** worksheet, calculate the statistical values listed below for each of the following sets of data: age, weight, height, initial triglyceride level, 3-month triglyceride level, 6-month triglyceride level, as well as for the dosage, percent change, and delta values you generated. Highlight this data to make the values easy to identify, and display no more than two decimal places.

   - Mean
   - Median
   - Standard deviation
   - Minimum value
   - Maximum value

4. In a column next to the patient data, calculate the ranking of the participants relative to their 6-month percent change in triglyceride levels. The rank of 1 should correspond to the participant with the greatest percent change.

Summary

1. On a separate worksheet titled **Summary**, create a small table that lists the total number of participants in each protocol by gender (male, female) and the total for the group. Include, by protocol and gender, the average 3-month and 6-month percent changes, and the average 3-month and 6-month delta for all participants. Identify this sheet with a yellow tab. Format the data to display no more than two decimal places and as percents where appropriate.

2. In an area below this summary information, briefly explain which protocol you recommend and why. Additionally, calculate the average number of milligrams per day per person for this chosen protocol.

3. Sort the **Data** worksheet by rank, and then filter the data to only display your chosen protocol.

C. Data Analysis Tools

Another way to look at this data is to graphically view the values grouped into categories.

1. Create a new worksheet named **Histogram**. Use a red tab color for this worksheet. Create Histogram with a chart output based on the 6-month delta data for the protocol you have chosen. Use these bin groupings: 10, 0, –10, –20, –30, –40, –50, –60, –70.

2. The research team frequently asks for the makeup of the participant group. On the same **Histogram** worksheet, create a histogram that describes the age distribution of the entire group, using all protocols. Organize the groupings at 10-year intervals, between 20 and 80.

D. Share Your Results

1. Since a large number of other research groups are interested in seeing the preliminary results of the study, you have been directed to make the data Internet-ready. Save the Summary table that you created in HTML format. The Web page should be entitled **Zobo Research Data.htm**.

2. In addition to making your summary information available, you have been asked to save the original data and your calculations on the **Data** worksheet in comma-delimited format. Name the file **Zobo.csv**.

E. Automate Data Acquisition

During the course of importing and combining this data you learned a few things about how to improve and streamline the process. You've spoken with the trial coordinators at each of the hospitals and they have agreed to standardize the file format you have used here on your data worksheet. Their files will contain the exact same columns and column order. From now on they will be sending you these comma-delimited files named **H1data.txt**, **H2data.txt**, and **H3data.txt**. These data files will not contain headings. Rather, the heading appears on your worksheet as in Figure 3.

FIGURE 3   Standardized Column Headings for Data

Hospital	SSN	Name	Age	M/F	Weight (lbs)	Height (in)	Drug Protocol	Initial - Triglycerides	3-mo. Triglycerides	6-mo. Triglycerides

Note that per your recommendation, the **Name** field contains the Last name followed by a space, followed by the middle initial. The data files do not contain headings; these already exist directly in your worksheet template.

Since you can now reliably count on a specific format, you have decided to automate the process as follows:

1. Create a new workbook **GetZobo.xls** that contains these headings and a macro named **GetData** that automatically imports all three comma-delimited text files at the same time.

2. When all of the information is imported, the macro should automatically sort the data by protocol and then by age (descending order).

3. Set the security level of the file so that the user is prompted upon opening the file as to whether or not to enable the macros.

4. Create a new button on the formatting toolbar that starts this macro. Use one of the floppy disk images as the button face.

5. Save the file without any imported data.

6. Make a copy of the **GetZobo.xls** workbook named **GetData1.xls** to test your macro. To test the automated process, each of the hospitals has sent some test data in the required format with the required file names. Import the data to the **GetData1.xls** file and save it with the test data.

F. Prepare a Budget for Phase Two Testing

One of your very next assignments is to prepare a budget for the 3-year trials that begin after approval of this first phase of human testing. You will prepare a budget based on the use of your selected protocol. If the protocol should change later, make sure your worksheet is flexible enough to be easily modified.

1. Begin your budget in a new workbook named **ZoboBudget.xls**. Prepare three identically formatted sheets, one for each year. Name your sheets **Year1**, **Year2**, and **Year3**.

2. Each sheet needs to contain the expenses for each of the items as listed in Figure 4. Expenses should be calculated for each of the twelve months and the yearly total. All expense values should be rounded to the nearest dollar. The input values that are required should appear as a separate input area at the top section of each worksheet.

FIGURE 4   Year One Expenses

Expense Item	Cost
Manufacturing and Distribution	$ 0.25 per milligram
Participant Fees	$25 per month per patient
Physician Fees	$1200 per patient per year
Blood Testing	$35 per participant per test (quarterly: January, April, July, October)
Urine Analysis	$5 per participant (bimonthly: January, March, May, etc.)
Administration and Overhead	$10,000 per month

To create this budget, you also make the following assumptions:

- Assume that there will initially be 1000 participants with an attrition rate of 5% per year (thus year two's budget is based on 950 participants). This value should be explicitly listed on the top portion of each year's budget as should all of the other inputs.

- Assume that each year has 365 days, and each month contains the corresponding number of days. (January 31, February 28, etc.)

- Assume that physician fees and blood and urine test fees increase approximately 5% percent per year.

- Assume all other fees will remain the same.

- For calculation purposes, assume that the average daily dosages per person per day match those of your selected protocol. Link this value to the **Zobo.xls** workbook, so any later changes can be automatically reflected in the budget when the file is opened.

3. Generate monthly and yearly totals for each expense item. Include a grand total for all expenses in each year.

4. After the budget for each year is complete, add a fourth worksheet titled **Summary**. This worksheet needs to contain the yearly total columns from each of the three years. Create 3-year totals by expense item. Include a grand total for the three years of expenses. Reference the values on the yearly worksheets, so any updates to the expenses for a given year are immediately reflected on the **Summary** worksheet.

5. Modify the budget to reflect new information. Due to a change in funding, the research team has asked you to modify this budget to reflect an initial participant group of 500, instead of the original 1000.

6. Use a new worksheet in the **Zobobudget.xls** file to create a chart that summarizes the percent of each component cost for this 3-year study based on the new group size. Your chart should contain labels and dollar values, as well as a title. Save the file with these updated values. Label this worksheet **Chart**.

PROJECT RESULTS

When you have completed the project, you should have the following files:

Zobo.xls, containing worksheets: **Data**; **Reject**; **Dosage**; **Summary**; **Histogram**

Zobo Research Data.htm

Zobo.csv

GetZobo.xls

GetData1.xls

ZoboBudget.xls, containing worksheets: **Year1**; **Year2**; **Year3**; **Summary**; **Chart**

SCIENCE CLASS GRADE BOOK

PROBLEM STATEMENT

As a newly hired science teacher at Nova Middle School, you need a way to keep track of grades for the students in each of your classes. After a discussion with your colleagues regarding the various methods of recording grades, you decide it would be best to create a custom grade workbook using Microsoft Excel to keep track of grades for your students. This computerized method of handling student grades is becoming more preferred than the standard, paper grade book, and you would like to benefit from the conveniences of an electronic copy, such as increased security, quicker averaging of grades, and greater reporting functionality.

AVAILABLE DATA

Data Files: **gradebook.csv**

One of your colleagues has offered you sample data to use when setting up your grade book and sent it to you as a comma-delimited file.

TASKS

A. Create the New Grade Book

First you have to create the new file for your grade book and import the sample data.

1. Open a new Microsoft Excel file and save it as **gradebook.xls**.

2. Import the data from the comma-delimited file **gradebook.csv**.

   - Place the data in the existing worksheet, beginning at cell A3.
   - Use the text data format for the first three columns (Student ID, First Name, and Last Name).
   - Use the general data format for the remaining columns.

3. Change the name of the current worksheet (tab) to **Science Grades**. Enter the title **Grade Book for** followed by (**your name**) at the top of the worksheet.

4. Freeze the panes of the worksheet so that the column headings and students' names and ID numbers are always visible.

B. Set up Data Calculations

Now that the workbook is set up, you need to enter the calculations.

1. Implement conditional formatting so that all zero grades are displayed in red.

2. In a column to the right of the sample data, calculate each student's average based on the grade weights in Figure 1. Title this column **Average**. Create a lookup table containing the grade weights on the **Science Grades** worksheet, and use absolute cell references to this table in the formula you create to compute the averages. This allows you to update your grade weights in one place, and you won't need to modify multiple formulas if the grade weights change.

3. In cells C15, C16, and C17, respectively, enter the row headings, **Average**, **Maximum**, and **Minimum**, and perform those calculations, copying the formula across columns D through P.

FIGURE 1   Grade Weights

Component	Grade Weight
Tests	45%
Homework	25%
Lab Reports	10%
Participation	10%
Attendance	10%

4. In the column to the right of **Average**, calculate each student's letter grade (from their average), along with the average course grade in cell Q15, based on the grading scale in Figure 2. Title this column **Letter Grade**. Create a lookup table containing the grade weights on your worksheet, and use absolute cell references to this table in the formula you create to compute the averages.

FIGURE 2   Grade Scale

Average	Letter Grade
>90.00%	A
80.00%–89.99%	B
70.00%–79.99%	C
60.00%–69.99%	D
<60.00%	F

5. Create a 3-D pie chart on a new sheet named **Grade Distribution**, depicting the distribution of letter grades. Use data labels and an appropriate chart title.

C. Filter the Data

In order to make the data easy to work with, you decide to automate the filtering process to make it easy to see the students' grades and the grade distribution.

1. On the **Science Grades** worksheet, set the column widths to AutoFit. Format the worksheet so that it is professional and easy to read.

2. On a new worksheet named **PivotTable & Chart**, create a PivotTable and PivotChart depicting each student's average, as well as an option to easily display the students receiving each of the five letter grades, by Student ID. The PivotChart should be a graphical illustration of the PivotTable. (*Note:* The PivotTable example in Figure 3 shows sample data which will not mirror your results.)

FIGURE 3   Sample PivotTable Displaying Students' Average Grade

	A	B	C
1	Letter Grade	(All) ▼	
2			
3	Average of Average		
4	Student ID ▼	Total	
5	175839	61	
6	189574	63	
7	308678	86	
8	371093	94	
9	564783	93	
10	578093	82	
11	637985	78	
12	727859	87	
13	754893	91	
14	947584	79	
15	Grand Total	81	
16			

D. Use Your Grade Book

Now that your grade calculations and tables are in place, you want the grade book to be simple to use and easy to keep up to date. Additionally, you want to be able to search for information quickly.

1. Use an AutoFilter to allow the quick filtering of data in columns A through O in the **Science Grades** worksheet.

2. Assign a unique tab color for each of the worksheet tabs in your workbook.

3. Create a macro, to be stored in this workbook, which automatically refreshes the data in the PivotTable. Name this macro **pivotRefresh** and set the shortcut key combination to **Ctrl+R**. Enter a relevant description in the Record Macro dialog box.

4. Define a cell range name for the range of cells representing the students' grades for Test 1. Accept the default name for this cell range. Repeat this process for the columns Test 2 through Average, accepting the default range names. Revise the formulas in the average, maximum, and minimum calculations (cell range D15:P17) to reflect the named ranges instead of the alphanumeric cell references.

5. Group the **Science Grades** and **Pivot Table & Chart** worksheets. Enter the text, **Created by:** (*Your Name*) in cell A25 and the current date in A26. Ungroup the two worksheets.

E. Allow Access to Your Grade Book

As part of your classroom duties, you are going to host a student teacher next term. You'd like him or her to be able to enter grades into your grade book, but you want to be able to review the entries. Additionally, as part of your work on the Education & the Internet committee at the school, you've volunteered to allow students to calculate their class averages on the school's intranet site as a pilot project.

1. Since the student teacher will be using this grade book to enter grades for your students, you want to keep track of each change that is made to the file. Configure the workbook to track all changes.

2. Create an interactive Web page that allows students to easily calculate their average via the Web. Do not include any student information or an individual student's grades on this Web page; they must type that in themselves. Save this page as **calc_average.mht**.

PROJECT RESULTS |

Upon completing this project, you should have the following files:

    gradebook.xls containing worksheets: **Science Grades**; **PivotTable & Chart**

    calc_average.mht

XDT SECURITY

PROBLEM STATEMENT

Congratulations! You have been hired by XDT's California regional office. XDT is one of the biggest home and business security corporations in the nation. Your new boss has outlined some initial tasks he would like you to begin working on. These include:

- Analysis of XDT's pricing structure for the Sacramento, California, field branch by customer and by customer class

- Creation of new data entry forms including one that allows telephone operators to easily access customer data and record incidents

- Creation of new reports to help management in monitoring customer fees and false alarms during specific high-alarm periods

- Creation of a user interface for the current Access database

To complete these initial tasks, he has given you a sample of the company's data to work with (**XDT.mdb**). This data is specific to the Sacramento, California, field office where they use the MS Access DBMS software. The types of analyses and database improvements you will be working on will be used as a model for a national system which is being considered. First, take a look at the current database and the included tables.

AVAILABLE DATA

Data Files: **XDT.mdb**

Customers

This is a listing of all customers (business and residential) with whom the company has active contracts or has had contracts in the past that are now inactive. It includes:

- **CustomerID**: A unique ID number associated with this customer.
- The customer's name (**FName** and **LName**) and address information including **Street**, **City**, **State**, and **Zip Code**.
- **Residential**: A Yes/No field indicating if this customer is a residential customer (Yes), or a business (No).

- ***Class***: This is a numeric value indicating a customer's pricing category. This number is based on several factors including the size of the building, the neighborhood crime level and/or the contents of the building.
- ***Active***: This is a Yes/No field indicating if this is an active customer. An active customer is someone who is currently contracting the services of XDT. The other customers are old customers who have decided to no longer use XDT's services.

Employees

This is a listing of all employees in the Sacramento XDT branch. These are the employees who are responsible for recording each call that XDT receives, notifying the proper authorities, and initiating any additional investigations if warranted. The table includes a unique employee ID number (***EmpID***) and the employee's first name (***Name***).

Calls

This is a log of all calls received by XDT in the previous year. Any time an alarm goes off, an employee must be sent to investigate the call. After investigating, the employee records the following information:

- ***Customer***: The customer ID of the building from which this alarm call originated (this is the same as ***CustID*** in the **Customers** table)
- ***Date***: The date of the call
- ***AnsweredBy***: The ID number of the employee who answered this call
- ***FalseAlarm***: A Yes/No field indicating whether this call was a false alarm (Yes) or an actual emergency (No)

TASKS

A. Set Relationships and Validate Records

Before you begin your analysis you need to make sure you have a valid set of data and that the information is properly related.

1. Set up the appropriate relationships between the tables based on the information you have already been given.

2. Enforce referential data integrity for each relationship. If referential data integrity is violated, find the unmatched records using a query and then delete those records using Update Query. If such queries are needed, name and save these queries. In this way you can reuse the queries if and when additional analyses are required. Remember to name the queries so their functions can be easily identified.

B. Analyze Customer Data

Now you are ready to analyze XDT's income by client. Ultimately this information will allow you to determine the basis of XDT's revenue and identify large-volume customers.

Extract Active Customer Information

1. Write a query or set of queries to create a list of the following information. Be sure to include only currently active customers. Name the Query **ActiveCustomersSummary**.

FIGURE 1   Results of Query(s)

ActiveCustomersSummary : Select Query				
Cust ID	Residential	Class	FalseAlarmQty	EmergencyQty

- **FalseAlarmQty** is the number of false alarms reported by this customer.
- **EmergencyQty** is the number of actual emergencies (calls that were not false alarms) reported by this customer.
- If a customer does not have calls in either of these categories, the query should return a zero value.

Analyze Prior Year's Fees

Calculate the fees accrued last year by each active customer based on the pricing structure described below. The accrued fees include a base fee per call and a false-alarm fee. In cases where customers have no alarm calls, a minimum idle fee is applied. To calculate the fees complete the following steps:

1. Add a table named **BaseFee** to the database listing the base fees per call. This fee per call is based on the customer's class. Classes are determined based on size, location, and contents. Include all of the information listed in Figure 2.

FIGURE 2   Base Fee Table

Class	BaseFee	Description
1	$ 50.00	2000 square feet or less
2	$ 75.00	2001–3000 sq. ft.
3	$125.00	3001–5000 sq. ft.
4	$200.00	5001–10,000 sq. ft. low crime area
5	$250.00	5001–10,000 sq. ft. high crime area
6	$300.00	under 10,000 sq. ft. and high value contents on premises
7	$500.00	over 10,000 sq. ft.

2. Write a query or set of queries that calculate the following information for each active customer (by customer ID). Name the query with the final values **FeeTotals** and format these values as currency. Include the customer's residential status and class.

- **BaseFees** are the fees assigned to this customer for all calls received from them (covers both false alarms and emergencies).
- **FAFee** (false alarm): To discourage customers from making false alarms, an additional fee is applied to the base if a call is a false alarm. Residential customers pay an FA fee of $75.00 per call. Business fee customers pay $300.00 per call.

- **IdleFee**: There are costs associated with maintaining accounts, even for customers who have made no calls in the past year. These costs include personnel handling the phones, the equipment provided at the locations, and so on. To cover these costs, XDT charges an idle fee for such accounts. This $45.00 idle fee is applied to only those customers who have had no calls during the past year.

- **TotalFees**: Calculate the total amount charged (total revenues) to the client for last year's calls (base fee, false alarm fee, and idle fee). Format this value as currency with no decimal places.

3. Calculate the grand totals for each fee (base, false alarm, and idle) and for the total fees charged. Name the query **GrandTotals.**

Generate Summary Information

1. Calculate the following summary information for each customer class (1 through 7) in a query using a PivotTable view. Name the query **PivotTotals.** Display totals only.

   - Calculate the total revenues from business customers by customer class.
   - Calculate the total revenues from residential customers by customer class.
   - Calculate the total revenues for all customers by customer class.

C. Create Data Entry Forms

Now that you have extracted the types of information that management has requested, they would like you to modify the database to make it accessible to staff receiving the emergency calls and to the sales team. To provide staff access, you need to set up several user forms.

Enter New Employees

1. Create a new form called **NewEmployees** that allows staff members to input new employee information. For reasons of privacy, this form should allow no deletions or editing of existing employee records; these tasks will be handled separately at a later date.

Enter New Customers

1. Create a new form named **NewCustomer** that allows the sales team to input new customer information.

   - Customer name fields should be displayed in alphabetical order (*Last, First*).

2. Allow staff to view, edit, or delete customer data using this form.

Enter New Calls

1. Create a new form named **CallsForm** that allows an operator to enter new call information and edit existing call information. Once a caller has been identified, the operator can bring up all relevant information about the location.

2. Model your form after the one displayed in Figure 3. The main part of the form should include information on each customer (including their full name and address).

FIGURE 3   Call Entry Form

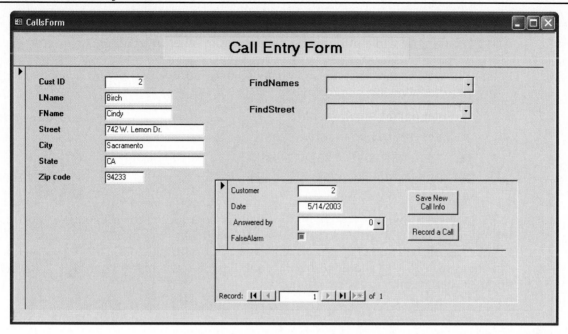

3. The main form should include two Find boxes, one to find the records based on the customer name, the other to find the records based on the customer's street address. These Find boxes should both automatically be updated when a new record is displayed. (*Hint*: Edit the VB code of the combo boxes to include a statement in each updating the other value to match the Customer ID.)

4. Include a subform which allows you to display all call information on the selected customer, one record at a time.

   - Add control buttons that allow operators to add and save a new record.
   - Set the default date to the current date.
   - Create a combo box that allows the operator to select his or her name from a list and store their ID in the **Answered by** field on the calls table.

5. Hide the navigation buttons on the main form only.

D. Create Reports for Management

In addition to the data entry forms, you have also been asked to create several reports to assist management.

1. Create a new report called **FeeTotals** that allows users to view both the detail and summary information that you generated with your **FeeTotals** query. List by customer their base fees, false alarm fees, idle fees, and total fees. Create a subtotal for each class of customer including the total value of each of these fees and the average values.

2. Management would like to know if there is an increase in false alarm calls during the summer months. Create a second report named **FalseAlarms** to list all false alarm calls during the months of June through September. List the customer number, name, zip code, and date of the call. Sort the list by zip code and then by date. Include a calculated field in the report footer listing the total number of false alarms during this period.

E. Create an Automated User Interface

Management would like to go even further in making this database system easy for the clerical staff to use while minimizing their access to other information.

1. Set up a switchboard that automatically opens when the database is opened and gives the user the following menu choices:

   - Enter or edit an alarm call.
   - Enter new customer information.
   - Enter new employee information.
   - Management Reports.
   - Close the database.

   Each of these menu items should launch the appropriate form, report, or action. The Management Reports option should open a sub-switchboard that allows the user to choose from either of the two preset reports that were written or return to the main switchboard. The main switchboard should also contain a Close the switchboard option. Use the default options when naming the switchboards.

PROJECT RESULTS

At the completion of this project, **XDT.mdb** should minimally contain the following objects:

Tables: **BaseFee**; **Calls**; **Customers**; **Employees**

Queries: **ActiveCustomerSummary**; **FeeTotals**; **GrandTotals**

Forms: **NewEmployees**; **NewCustomer**; **CallsForm**

Reports: **FalseAlarms**; **FeeTotals**

Additional objects may be necessary to complete this project.

SNORTING ELK RESORT EMERGENCY CLINIC

PROBLEM STATEMENT

Recently retired from their positions as trauma surgeons in a large metropolitan hospital, Holly and Henry McRae have decided to share a position as the on-call doctor at the emergency clinic for the Snorting Elk Resort, an all-season resort high in the Montana Rockies.

Holly and Henry find that the clinic currently uses only paper records to record what patient information can be obtained from the injury victim, the record of aid provided, and the conditions under which the accident occurred. You have been hired by the resort for both your snowboarding and your database skills. Friday through Sunday, you are an on-mountain ambassador for skiing and snowboarding guests. Wednesday and Thursday your job is to help Holly and Henry plan, design, create, and use an automated injury-tracking system.

AVAILABLE DATA

Data Files: **Employee.mdb**; **Injury Records.xls**; **Patient Records.xls**

Registration

Registration information is collected when an injury victim is brought to the clinic. Henry and Holly want to create a way for this information to be entered directly into the clinic's database.

FIGURE 1   Snorting Elk Registration Form

Snorting Elk Resort Emergency Clinic
REGISTRATION FORM

(Please Print)

Today's Date ____/____/____

PATIENT INFORMATION

Patient's Last Name	First	Middle

Is this your legal name?	If not, what is your legal name?	(Former Name)	Birth Date	Age	Sex
❑ Yes ❑ No			/ /		❑ M ❑ F

Street Address	City	State	ZIP Code	Social Security	Home Phone No.
					( )

How arrived at the Clinic (Please check on box)

❑ Walk-in   ❑ Ski Patrol   ❑ Search & Rescue   ❑ Resort Employee   ❑ Other

Name of Resort Employee

INSURANCE INFORMATION

Person Responsible for Bill	Address (if different)	Home Phone No.

Is this patient covered by insurance?   ❑ Yes   ❑ No   ( )

❑ Self-pay   ❑ Insurance (list)

❑ Other

First Aid

First aid information is collected by the rescuers of the victim and updated in the clinic. Henry and Holly want to add a field to track who is recording the information on the form.

FIGURE 2   Snorting Elk First Aid Record

Snorting Elk Resort
FIRST AID RECORD

(Please Print)

Today's Date ____/____/____   Time ____:____AM PM

INJURY INFORMATION

Last Name	First	Middle

Incident/Injury #

Time							
Pulse							
B/P Upper							
B/P Lower							
Temperature							

Ski Patrol

Minor injuries are often handled by the Ski Patrol. (For all accidents, the Ski Patrol gathers the following information: first and last names of the victims; their birthdates and genders; the dates, times, and locations of the accidents; the types of equipment the victims were using; and the types of injury.)

TASKS

A. Design the Database

In order to build the database that Henry and Holly are requesting, you first need to understand the data. Review the fields, assess the relationships between the data, and develop appropriate tables.

1. Refer to the **Registration and First-Aid** forms and the **Patient Records** worksheet to determine which fields are necessary.

2. Using a worksheet or word-processing program (or pen and paper), create a list of all the fields, specifying the field name, data type, and properties of each.

3. Create an entity relationship diagram using paper and pencil or an appropriate drawing program to show the flow of data through the database. Use the format illustrated in Figure 3.

FIGURE 3   Sample Section of Entity Relationship Diagram

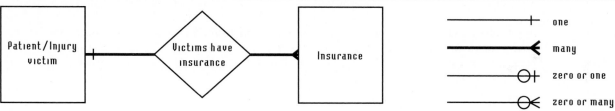

4. Use the following business rules to help determine the table relationships:

   - A patient may have zero or more insurance companies.
   - A patient may have zero or more billing addresses (the home and billing address are the same).
   - A patient may have one or more injuries.
   - A patient may have one or more aid records.
   - An insurance company may have zero or more patients.

5. By applying the rules of data normalization, divide your list of fields into appropriate tables. Next to each field you identified, add the appropriate table name.

6. Document intersection tables as appropriate to establish links between tables.

7. Create a new database named **Emergency Clinic.mdb**.

B. Import Patient Data into the Database

Now that you have designed the structure of the **Emergency Clinic.mdb** database, it's time to import the clinic's data.

1. Import the **Patient Records.xls** worksheet into the **Emergency Clinic.mdb** database.

2. Create Make-table queries to split the **Patient Records** table into the tables according to your database design.

3. Write Delete queries to clean up the tables after they are created to remove redundant fields and blank rows.

4. Modify the tables using the appropriate data types, field sizes, captions, formats, and input masks.

5. Create any other tables needed, and set a primary key for each table.

C. Link to the Employee Database

Holly wants to make certain that the names of the employees are always consistent. The HR department has agreed to allow the clinic to link to the **Employee.mdb** database.

1. Link to the tables in the **Employee.mdb** database that you need to create the lookups.

2. Design a way to look up the names in the **Admitted By** field in the **Patient** table and the **Recorder** field in the **Aid Log** table. Create the lookups so that the **Admitted By** lookup displays all employees and the **Recorder** lookup displays only the Clinic and Ski Patrol employees. Additionally, display the first and last name in one field and do not show the employee number.

D. Import Ski Patrol Data into the Database

Henry and Holly would also like to be able to match the injury victims with the records kept by the Ski Patrol on the type of equipment involved in and the location of the accident. These records are kept in an Excel spreadsheet and need to be imported into the database.

1. Import the **Injury Records.xls** worksheet into the **Emergency Clinic.mdb** database.

2. Create an Unmatched query to determine if there are any records in the **Injury Records** table that do not exist in your new **Patient** table. (*Hint*: Change **Is Null** to **Is Not Null** in the criteria row after running the query. Now you can use this edited query to go on to the next steps.)

3. Modify the query to add the patient's SSN and remove the redundant fields.

4. Change the query to a Make-table query to create a new normalized table named **Injury**.

5. Modify the table using the appropriate data types, field sizes, captions, formats, and input masks.

6. Set a primary key for the table.

7. Delete the **Patients** and **Injuries** tables when you are certain the data is correct in the new table.

E. Minimize Data Entry Error

Holly is concerned about the validity of the data and wants to make sure that injuries and billing addresses cannot get into the database without being related to a patient. She also wants to make certain that a when a patient record is updated all related records are updated; however, she does not want to be able to delete a patient and all related records.

1. Open the Relationships window and establish referential integrity between the tables.

2. Set Cascade Update and Cascade Delete options to conform to Holly's wishes.

3. Create and print the Relationship report.

F. Create the Admission Form

Holly would like a form that allows the clinic employees to enter all the patient information using just one form. Figure 4 shows a sample admission form.

FIGURE 4   Sample Admission Form

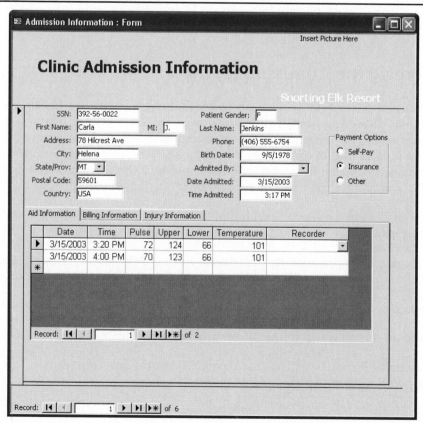

1. Create the queries you need to use in the subforms on the pages for the tab controls.

2. Create a query for the Insurance tab that allows you to lookup the patient's insurance company from a drop down list. When the company is selected, all the address information is automatically entered.

3. Create the form and test it to make certain that you can enter a new patient with billing information and an insurance company.

4. You need to manually input the First Aid Log information (Figure 5) for each patient.

FIGURE 5   First Aid Log

First Name	Last Name	Date	Time	Pulse	Upper	Lower	Temp	Recorder
Carla	Jenkins	3/15/2003	3:20 PM	72	124	66	101	Holly MacRae
Carla	Jenkins	3/15/2003	4:00 PM	70	123	66	101	Holly MacRae
John	Moore	4/1/2003	8:44 AM	70	108	64	100	Henry MacRae
John	Moore	4/1/2003	9:00 AM	68	105	53	99	Henry MacRae
Jack	Szmansky	4/10/2003	9:35 AM	76	130	80	99	Debi Greggs
Jack	Szmansky	4/10/2003	10:00 AM	70	125	78	99	Holly MacRae
Thom	Howard	4/11/2003	12:05 PM	63	110	64	99	Holly MacRae
Danni	George	4/12/2003	1:12 PM	50	96	54	99	Debi Greggs
Danni	George	4/12/2003	2:00 PM	50	95	55	99	Holly MacRae
Greta	Schelvis	4/8/2003	3:18 PM	48	98	58	99	Henry MacRae

G. Customize the Admission Form

Holly and Henry think the new form is great; however, they would like a couple of changes to make data input easier and more accurate. The lookup query works great on the Insurance tab for companies already in the database. Holly and Henry would like you to add a button that opens a form to add a new company. Holly noticed that some staff members try to enter insurance information even if the client does not have insurance. She wants you to have the Insurance tab appear only when the patient has insurance.

1. Create a form for adding additional insurance companies, and place a Close button on the form.

2. Create a macro to open the **Insurance** form in Add Mode. Assign the macro to a command button on the Insurance tab of the **Admission Information** form.

3. Add a field to the **Patient** table to record payment options.

4. Add an option group to the **Admission Information** form to track payment options.

5. Create VBA code to set the visible property for the Insurance tab to True only when the option for insurance has been selected.

H. Make the Data Accessible on the Intranet

Henry is often at the Ski Patrol building and needs to access certain pieces of information via the resort's intranet. Additionally, Holly would like injury data available on the intranet to allow easy access for management.

1. Create a data access page to allow Henry to access the name of each patient and their related first aid information. Title this Web page **Patient Aid**.

2. Create a PivotChart for Holly that allows her to filter by Gender to show *Equipment* as the category field and *Injury Type* as the series field. Count on the *Last Name* field. Title this Web page **Injuries by Gender Chart**.

3. Create a PivotTable for Holly that allows her to filter by Location. Use *Equipment* and *Injury Type* as the column and row fields. Use *Date* as the details field. Title this Web page **Injury Analysis PivotTable**.

I. Make the Database Easy to Use

Holly and Henry are pleased with the work that you have done so far. They would like you to add one last touch to the database. They want to be able to quickly get to the database forms they use.

1. Create a form to use as the switchboard and create the following buttons:

   - Add a new patient using the **Admission/Information** form.
   - Edits a patient's information using the **Admission/Information** form.
   - Open the PivotTable.
   - Open the PivotChart.
   - Exit the switchboard.
   - Exit the database.

2. Set the properties on the switchboard to remove the navigation buttons, scroll bars, and minimize and restore buttons. Also make sure that the switchboard cannot be resized.

PROJECT RESULTS |

When you have completed this database, you should have the following databases and files:

Emergency Clinic.mdb containing, at minimum, the following objects (additional objects may be necessary to complete the project):

Tables: **Patient; Injury**

Forms: **Admission Information**

Employee.mdb

Injuries by Gender Chart.html

Injury Analysis PivotTable.html

Patient Aid.html

Patient Aid_files folder

IT DEPARTMENT, HUNTINGTON UNIVERSITY

PROBLEM STATEMENT

When Katherine Michael, Huntington University's Director of IT operations, found the funds to upgrade most of her school's computer desktops, she needed to determine which computers to replace. Unfortunately, she lacked an easy way to identify the computers she needed to upgrade.

You have been approached by Katherine and tasked with finding a solution to her problem. Currently, the University does have a database with an inventory of all of the computers on campus with their location and some of the specific hardware and software components of those computers. This database currently consists of a single table with that inventory. Therefore, you need to add new tables, along with queries, forms, and reports, to make the database useful for determining which computers are in need of upgrades.

AVAILABLE DATA

Data Files: **ComputerInventory.mdb**; **Employee_Entries.xls**; **HuntingtonITCenterEmployees.xls**; **Computer_History.xls**; **Upgrade_Information.xls**

Use the **ComputerInventory.mdb** database as a starting point for your work. The only table in the database, **Computer Inventory**, may be modified as needed to complete the project for Katherine. Figure 1 shows some of the fields in the table.

FIGURE 1   Computer Inventory Sample Data

ComputerID	Manufacturer	Model	DatePurchased	Building	Room	ContactPerson	RAM	HD	CPU	OS
1	Dell	GX110	2/1/2002	PH	110	Wilma James	128	40	800	98
2	Dell	GX110	2/1/2002	PH	215	Brent Jacobs	128	40	800	98
3	Dell	GX110	2/1/2002	CH	311	Jenna Myers	128	40	800	98
4	Dell	GX110	2/1/2002	GH	097	Brian McAffery	128	40	800	98
5	Dell	GX110	2/1/2002	CH	192	James Johnson	128	40	800	98
6	Dell	GX110	2/1/2002	PH	214	Katie Morgan	128	40	800	98

Before beginning the tasks Katherine requested, you need to thoroughly review the **Computer Inventory** table to become familiar with its structure and data. Figure 2 shows some sample fields and their properties.

FIGURE 2   Computer Inventory Fields and Properties

Field Name	Data Type	Description
ComputerID	AutoNumber	ID number assigned to new computer desktops
Manufacturer	Text	Manufacturer from who the computer was purchased
Model	Text	Model number of the computer system purchased
DatePurchased	Date/Time	Date that the computer was purchased
Building	Text	Building where the computer is located
Room	Text	Room in which the comptuer is located
ContactPerson	Text	Person who is in charge of the computer
RAM	Text	MB of RAM installed
HD	Text	Size, in gigabytes, of the hard drive installed in the computer
CPU	Text	Speed, in MHz, of the CPU of the computer
OS	Text	Windows operating system version installed on the computer system

TASKS

A. Restructuring the Database

A major problem with the current database is that there is only one table that contains all of the information for the computers contained on campus. Take some time to think about other fields that may be needed in this table and how this table can be normalized and combined with your additional data for a better design. Some of the particular data items that you might want to add include employees of the IT center who enter the computers into the database, a history table showing computers that have been put out of service, and a table containing individual upgrades made to computers without replacing the entire computer.

1. You have been given a listing of IT center employees and their IDs in an Excel workbook, **HuntingtonITCenterEmployees.xls**. Import the employee data into an **Employees** table.

2. Add a field to the current **Computer Inventory** table to identify which employee entered the computer into the database. The IDs of the employees who have entered the current set of computers in inventory can be found in **Employee_Entries.xls**.

3. Create a **History** table where information about computers removed from the current inventory can be stored. In this table, be sure to include the same information stored in the **Computer Inventory** table, but add an additional field (labeled **Date_Removed**) that captures the date the computer was removed from service. **Computer_History.xls** contains a short listing of computers that have already been removed from current inventory.

4. Create a table for computer upgrades titled **Upgrades**. This table tracks upgrades to computers, based on that computer's ID from the **Computer Inventory** table. Additional information that needs to be captured for each upgrade includes: the ID of the computer upgraded, a description of the upgrade, the date of the upgrade, and the cost of the upgrade. A listing of upgrades made to current computers in inventory can be imported from the **Upgrade_Information.xls** spreadsheet.

B. Determine How to Identify Computers Needing Replacement

To make the data contained in your database useful, you need to create several queries for Katherine to access. These queries can be used to locate computers with specific elements that need to be upgraded.

1. The three queries that Katherine has specifically stated that she wants are:

- **Upgrades Based on CPU**: Displays the manufacturer, model, and location of all computers that have a CPU whose speed in MHz is less than a certain value. This value should be entered at the time the query is run by the user of the database.

- **Upgrades Based on RAM**: Displays the manufacturer, model, and location of all computers that have RAM that is smaller in size than a certain value. This value should be entered at the time the query is run by the user of the database.

- **Upgrades Based on hard drive**: Displays the manufacturer, model, and location of all computers that have a hard drive smaller than a certain value. This value should be entered at the time the query is run by the user of the database.

2. You recommend three additional queries to Katherine that you believe can make the database more useful:

- **Computers by Building**: Displays a listing of all computers found within a given building

- **Employee Entries**: Displays a list of all computers that have been entered into the database by a given employee, whether the computer is in the current inventory table or the history table

- **Total Expenditures**: Shows the sum of all money spent on computer purchases and upgrades. This query needs to take into account the monetary values within the **Computer Inventory**, **Upgrades**, and **History** tables. (*Hint*: You may need to use a Union query to develop this query successfully.)

C. Aggregate the Data

Katherine mentions that she would like to be able to access some aggregate information. You offer to create some queries for her that aggregate the data in simple, easy-to-read formats.

1. Create a query named **Upgrades Based on Date Purchased**. This query displays the number of computers in each building that were purchased more than four years before the current date compared to the total number of computers in those buildings. (*Hint*: Use a crosstab query.)

2. Create a query named **Purchases by Building** that lists the number of computers contained within each building and show how much money was spent per building. A representation of what the result of this query should look like is shown in Figure 3.

FIGURE 3   Sample Results for Purchases by Building Query

Building	Computers in the Building	Total Purchases for Building
PH	173	$311,400
CH	221	$309,400
DL	750	$1,312,500
...	...	...
TOTAL	3101	$4,961,600

3. Create a query named **Purchases by Year** that lists the total dollar amount per year spent on new computer purchases and upgrades on the Huntington campus. A representation of what the result of this query should look like is shown in Figure 4.

FIGURE 4   Sample Results for Purchases by Year Query

Year	Purchased Amount
2002	$752,010
2001	$625,000
...	...
TOTAL	$6,321,113

D. Automate Data Entry

One of Katherine's biggest needs for the database is to make data entry easy for the inexperienced Access user. She has asked for two forms to be added, including a form to add new computers to the inventory and a form to capture upgrades made to existing computers.

1. Create a form that can be used to enter new computer purchases from this date forward. Make sure to provide an area for entering data into each of the fields in the **Computer Inventory** table.

   Design the form so the data entry is as easy as possible by including a list box for the building location of the computers, populating it initially with the 2-letter abbreviations used for buildings on the Huntington campus: PH, CH, GH, DL, ML, JH, SH, and SC. Save the form as **New Computer Entry**.

2. Create a form that can be used to enter information regarding upgrades that have been installed in existing computers. Make sure to provide an area on the form for the recording of each of the data fields of the **Computer Upgrades** table created in an earlier task. Save the form as **Computer Upgrades Entry**.

E. Create Reports

Katherine wants reports that look professional and are easy to read and follow. In particular, she would like to have many of the queries that you created converted into reports that can be printed and viewed easily.

1. Design and create a report that shows the data found in the **Purchases by Building** query. Give the report a meaningful title and format the report with the Corporate style. Save the report as **Purchases by Building**.

2. Design and create a report that shows the data found in the **Purchases by Year** query. Give the report a meaningful title and format the report with the Corporate style. Save the report as **Purchases by Year**.

3. Using your knowledge of custom report design, create one other report that you feel would be useful to Katherine in her use of this database.

F. Provide Easy Access to the Data

To make access to the database features even easier, you are asked to provide an interface that is easy to use.

1. Create a switchboard that is displayed when the database is opened.

2. On the switchboard, create macro buttons which can be used to access each of the forms, queries, and custom reports that you have created for this database.

3. Create a macro, available from the switchboard, that allows a user to enter the ID number of a given computer in the **Computer Inventory** table, and move that computer from the current inventory into the **History** table.

4. Be sure to format the switchboard so that it appears professional and easy to use.

G. Make the Data Available to the Department

Because this database is to be used on multiple computers, it will need to be replicated. As not all the users are familiar with Access, the database should be set up to use the form you created as the interface.

1. Use Microsoft Windows Briefcase to make a replica of the completed database so that it can be shared among computers at the IT Help desk and Katherine's office.

2. Set the startup options to hide the database window and open the switchboard whenever the database is opened.

3. Be sure to include data validation for your tables to ensure users of the database are entering valid data. To enforce some of the data validation rules below, you may have to change the data types of the fields currently in the table or change the validation on the forms that input data into the tables. Specific validation rules should include:

   ■ Limit room number to between 100 and 999.
   ■ Ensure entered dates do not occur in the future (beyond the current date).

- Ensure that the CPU, hard drive size, and RAM values are integers only.
- Limit building names to their 2-letter abbreviations.

4. Thoroughly test all forms, queries, and reports against the data contained in the database to ensure they are returning accurate information.

PROJECT RESULTS |

At the completion of this project, **ComputerInventory.mdb** should contain the following objects:

Tables: **Computer Inventory**; **Employees**; **History**; **Upgrades**

(Queries: **Upgrades Based on Date Purchased**; **Purchases by Building**; **Purchases by Year**)

Forms: **New Computer Entry**; **Computer Upgrades Entry**

Reports: **Purchases by Building**; **Purchases by Year**

Additional objects may be necessary to complete the project.

NATIONAL EDUCATION CONFERENCE

PROBLEM STATEMENT

Congratulations! You have been selected to attend a national conference for educators and deliver a presentation covering the methods and advantages of incorporating PowerPoint into the classroom environment. Sharon Day, the conference organizer, informs you that teachers representing all grade levels will attend your session, so it is important that you cover topics that can be of use to the *entire* audience.

Since you are attempting to demonstrate the value of using PowerPoint in the classroom, you feel it is especially important to enhance your PowerPoint presentation to include some of the more advanced features of the program. Throughout your presentation, you want the audience to see samples of the types of effects they can produce using PowerPoint. You're hoping to generate enthusiasm in your audience for trying out PowerPoint when they return to their classrooms.

AVAILABLE DATA

Data Files: There are no starting data files for this project.

However, throughout the development of this presentation, you will be asked to find and include appropriate graphics and sound clips.

Web Sites: For relevant Web sites, visit the Student Online Companion at **www.course.com/downloads/sites/projects**.

TASKS

A. Develop an Original Slide Master and Title Master

You first want to capture the attention of your audience by creating an attractive slide show.

1. Create a new blank presentation and save it as **conference_pres.ppt**.

2. Customize the title master to your liking, but remember to consider the techniques you have learned for creating a well-designed PowerPoint presentation. On the title master, be sure to:

   - Include a background color or background image.
   - Include an eye-catching image in the foreground.

3. Customize the slide master to your liking. Keep things simple, but use a well-designed color scheme.

   - Use a custom image for your bullet points instead of the default bullet style.

B. Create the Content

Now it's time to add the substance of your presentation. Include not only what the audience will see on each slide, but also your personal notes to assist you while presenting.

1. Use a title slide layout for the first slide in your presentation. This slide should read **Incorporating PowerPoint in the Classroom** as the slide title, and your name as the subtitle.

2. Using the title and text slide layout for the second slide, include an appropriate slide title as well as an outline of the presentation topics you wish to cover. Additional information on PowerPoint can be found online. Check the Student Online Companion for related Web sites.

   Required topics for this presentation include (but are not limited to):

   - Brief background of yourself (to establish your credibility)
   - Overview of PowerPoint
   - When to use PowerPoint
   - Advantages and benefits of using PowerPoint for students and instructors
   - Disadvantages of using PowerPoint and suggestions for working around the disadvantages
   - Hardware and software required to run PowerPoint presentations in the classroom

3. Create the additional slides in your presentation that adequately address the topics of your presentation, as mentioned above. Be sure to use information you feel to be appropriate for a lecture of this nature.

   Include the following effects in your presentation:

   - Use at least three different slide layouts (in addition to the title and text layout).

- At least two of your slides must have clip art, one slide must contain an appropriate image downloaded from the Internet, and one slide must include a downloaded sound clip from the Internet. Provide the appropriate credit lines where appropriate. Refer to the Student Online Companion for relevant links.
- Use a table in one of your slides to creatively depict the hardware and software requirements for using PowerPoint.
- Survey at least ten teachers on whether they use multimedia presentations to enhance their lectures, do not use multimedia presentations to enhance their lectures, or wish to learn how to use multimedia presentations in the classroom. Format your results in a chart, in a type appropriate for comparing percentages of a total.

4. Add a slide summarizing your presentation topics, using the title and text layout.

5. Create a final slide to the presentation, using the title slide layout. This slide should look identical to your opening slide.

6. Add speaker notes to each of the slides to assist you in preparing for and delivering your presentation. Make sure to include at least three talking points per slide.

C. Set Presentation Options

Now that your content is in place, you decide to enhance the appearance and effectiveness of your presentation by adding additional display options, action items, and animation effects.

1. Use the custom animation feature on the slide master to add appropriate animation effects to your presentation.

2. Add a slide footer to each slide (except the title slides) containing the slide number, date (set to update automatically), and the text **Incorporating PowerPoint in the Classroom**.

3. Add appropriate slide transitions to the entire presentation.

4. Add hyperlinks to each of your presentation topics on the second slide of the presentation that, when clicked, take you to their respective area of the presentation. Remove the underline effect from these hyperlinks.

5. Using the slide master, add action buttons on each slide in the presentation that can take you forward and backward one slide at a time.

6. Use the PowerPoint Meeting Minder to allow you to create notes throughout the delivery of your presentation. These notes might include questions presented by your audience that you can't answer immediately and need time to research. You may also wish to record notes and ideas your audience might present to you.

7. Insert a pleasant CD audio track into the first and last slides of your presentation to give your audience something to listen to while waiting for your presentation to begin and at the conclusion of your presentation.

8. Create a self-running presentation by rehearsing your presentation and determining how much time you need to speak about each slide. Set up automatic timing to advance through your presentations according to the pace that works best for you.

D. Share the Presentation

Sharon asks you to send an outline of your presentation to share with the other presenters. Additionally, she also wants a handout that she can prepare for distribution to the audience members. During this discussion with Sharon, you volunteer to also submit your presentation Internet-ready so she can post it on the conference's Web site.

1. Save the changes to your presentation.

2. Print a copy of your presentation with three slides per page.

3. Export the presentation outline to a new Microsoft Word document. Save the word document as **ppt_outline.doc**.

4. Save the presentation as a Web page for submission to the conference organizer to post on their Web site. Name the file **ppt_web.htm**. Remember to preview your presentation in a Web browser to make sure that all your effects still work as you intended.

5. In case you are assigned to present in a room without adequate technology to display a PowerPoint presentation, design a copy of your presentation ideal for printing on overhead transparencies. Name the new presentation **ppt_overhead.ppt**.

6. You're hoping to generate a lot of publicity for your presentation at the conference. You decide to use your presentation slides to set up a single-page poster. Title this file **ppt_poster.ppt**. You don't have to print the poster; just create the format that could be sent to a service bureau for printing.

PROJECT RESULTS |

Upon completing this project, you should have the following files:

conference_pres.ppt

ppt_outline.doc

ppt_web.htm (and **ppt_web_files** folder)

ppt_overhead.ppt

ppt_poster.ppt

SUNSET FINANCIAL SERVICES

PROJECT OUTLINE

A. Create the Presentation and Master Slides

B. Create the Text and Add Designs and Animation

C. Create Controls for Kiosk Browsing

D. Record the Narration

E. Finalize the Presentation

PROBLEM STATEMENT

Sunset Financial Services is a regional accounting company and is participating in the local college's career fair. The director of human relations is very keen to hire graduating accounting college students. As the new marketing intern for Sunset Financial Services, you have been asked to develop a PowerPoint presentation that will be shown at the college fair.

Because there will only be one representative from Sunset attending the fair, the presentation needs to be a timed, looping presentation consisting of eight slides and narration that can be run through a Web browser. The HR director also wants to make sure that any interested student can stop and restart the presentation as they watch.

AVAILABLE DATA

Data Files: **Salary Scale.xls**; **sunset picture.jpg**

TASKS

A. Create the Presentation and Master Slides

The HR director provides you with some guidelines for the presentation design and a graphic file used on all of Sunset Financial Services' visual correspondence.

1. Use a Clouds presentation design for the Title Master. In the top-right corner, insert the **sunset picture.jpg** graphic. Resize as necessary.

2. Use a Clouds presentation design for the Slide Master, and put the company name, **Sunset Financial Services**, as the title for all slides. Save the presentation as **Sunset Financial Services.ppt**.

B. Create the Text and Add Designs and Animation

The HR director gives you her notes on what she wants you to cover in the presentation. She is familiar with PowerPoint and has suggestions for animations and text effects.

FIGURE 1   HR Director's Content Notes

Slide Number	Slide Text
Title Slide	Delete the subtitle box
Slide 2	Provides a variety of financial services: ■ Tax ■ Audit ■ Consulting ■ Bookkeeping
Slide 3	Create a pyramid diagram, where Bookkeeping appears on the bottom row; Consulting on the second; Audit on the third; and Tax on the top.
Slide 4	Insert file **Salary Scale.xls**
Slide 5	Jackie Chang, President ■ John Guys, Vice President Tax 　■ Christopher Parsons, Manager Corporate Tax 　■ Gary Humphreys, Manager Personal Tax ■ Kendra Sanchez, Vice President Audit 　■ Pauline Manucci, Manager Auditing ■ Kayleigh Smith, Vice President Consulting 　■ Timothy Crane, Manager Small Business Consulting 　■ Neil Cruz, Manager Corporate Consulting ■ George Hayes, Vice President Bookkeeping 　■ Martin Mendez, Manager Bookkeeping
Slide 6	■ Progressive company ■ Fast-track promotion opportunities ■ Regular salary increases ■ Travel opportunities
Slide 7	■ 100% employer paid health plan ■ Dental, vision, and life insurance plans ■ Tuition reimbursement ■ 401K retirement plan
Slide 8	Insert the text "We want to talk with you now! Sign up for interviews today!" inside a banner AutoShape

FIGURE 2   HR Director's Notes on Animations and Effects

Slide Number	Slide Treatment
Title Slide	Animate the title with Magnify animation
Slide 2	Animate with Circle animation
Slide 3	Animate the title with Ease In animation
Slide 4	Format the table appropriately
Slide 5	Create a hierarchical organizational chart, with a hanging layout; select the 3D color style for the chart
Slide 6	Animate the title with Ease In animation, and use a custom animation for the bullet points
Slide 7	Animate the title with Curve Up and the bullets with Wipe animation
Slide 8	Change the color of the banner to Sapphire on the preset gradient Fill Effects menu; make the text bold and large enough to fill the banner; animate the slide with spinner animation

C. Create Controls for Kiosk Browsing

Since this presentation will be available through a kiosk at the career fair, you need to add the controls to allow visitors to control the playing of the presentation.

1. Add the control buttons to the slides. The forward buttons should link to the next slide in the presentation and the backward button to the previous slide. Add a forward button to Slide 1. Add forward, back, and home buttons to slide 2 of the presentation. Slide 8 should have a back and home button only. The home button should link to the title slide.

2. Format each button so that it is ½ inch by ½ inch in size. Align the buttons at the bottom and distribute horizontally.

3. Group the buttons and copy the buttons from Slide 2 to Slides 3–7.

D. Record the Narration

The HR director has specified that the presentation also have narration. The visitors to Sunset's booth will be able to watch and listen to this presentation by themselves.

1. Record your narration, working from the notes given in Figure 3. When recording your narration, remember to speak clearly. Enunciation and pronunciation are the keys to a successful narration.

FIGURE 3   Notes on Narration

Slide Number	Recommended Narration
Slide 1	Sunset Financial Services is a regional accounting firm offering a variety of financial services.
Slide 2	Sunset Financial Services is currently recruiting forward-thinking college graduates for its four departments.
Slide 3	Sunset Financial Services is predominantly recruiting for bookkeepers and consultants, but we do have openings in audit and tax that need to be filled immediately.
Slide 4	We have been in business for 25 years and are proud to have given salary increases every year.
Slide 5	We are excited about our diverse employee population, and we have excellent, friendly managers in all four departments.
Slide 6	We are a progressive company, and we have a policy of promoting within.
Slide 7	We have an excellent benefits package, which includes a 100 percent employer-paid health plan.
Slide 8	Sunset Financial Services is anxious to talk to you. Please sign up today for an interview.

2. Set up the presentation to be a kiosk browsing presentation. Rehearse the timings to make sure the narration is not interrupted.

E. Finalize the Presentation

As you are reviewing the presentation one last time, the HR director stops by with an additional request: along with having the presentation run on a kiosk at the show, she also wants to post it to the company's Web site.

1. Save presentation as a Web document, titled **Sunset Financial Services.htm**.

PROJECT RESULTS

Upon completing this project, you should have the following files:

Sunset Financial Services.ppt

Sunset Financial Services.htm

Sunset Financial Services_files folder

FRANK'S MEXICAN RESTAURANT

PROBLEM STATEMENT

As manager of Frank's Mexican Restaurant, you have decided to develop a PowerPoint presentation to review the U.S. Department of Agriculture's Safe Food Handling recommendations. Because your restaurant is inspected by the Department of Health to make sure that it is clean and all safe food handling techniques are being followed, you need your employees to understand the guidelines.

You've already done the necessary research at the U.S. Department of Agriculture's Web site to get an understanding of what you need to cover. The U.S. Department of Agriculture divides Food Safety into four main groups: clean, separate, cook, and chill. Based on this information, you have decided to have slides covering these four topics. Now it's time to create the presentation from the information you've found.

AVAILABLE DATA

Data Files: **CookingMeat.xls**; **FoodSafety.jpg**; **CookThermo.jpg**

However, throughout the development of this presentation, you will be asked to create bullet points based on what you found on food safety web sites.

Web Sites: For relevant Web sites, visit the Student Online Companion at **www.course.com/downloads/sites/projects**.

TASKS |

A. Create Master and Title Slides

First, you want to create professional-looking slides that emphasize the seriousness and importance of the information you need to convey to your staff.

1. Create a new presentation and save it as **FranksMexicanRestaurant.ppt**.

2. Select the presentation design Pixel and customize the master slide by making all titles appear in bold and centered.

3. Create your first slide as a title slide. Make **Frank's Mexican Restaurant** the title and **Food Safety** the subtitle. Position the image, **FoodSafety.jpg**, in the lower-right corner of the slide.

B. Create Slides to Address Each Topic Area

Now you need to develop the bullet points for your presentation. You have already identified specific Web pages to assist you in developing your presentation. You'll find these sites listed on the Student Online Companion.

Clean

You have decided to create three slides (Slides 2–4) to address hand washing, as it is the most important topic; and one slide (Slide 5) to cover cleaning and disinfecting surfaces. Each slide is a Title and Text slide.

- Compose five bullet points on **Why Wash Your Hands** (Slide 2)
- Compose four bullets that explain **When Do You Wash Your Hands** (Slide 3)
- Compose four bullets points on **How You Wash Your Hands** (Slide 4)
- Compose five bullets to highlight how to **Clean and Disinfect Surfaces** (Slide 5)

Separate

Compose four bullets on **Cross Contamination** (Slide 6). Use a Title and Text slide.

Cook

Write four bullet points on why to **Use a Thermometer** (Slide 7), and insert the image, **CookThermo.jpg**, into the bottom-right corner of the slide. Use a Title and Text slide.

The next three slides (Slides 8–10) should be titled **Cooking Temperatures of Meat**. Using the data provided in **CookingMeat.xls** to create tables on all three slides to present this information.

For all of the tables, you want to bold the heading rows, merge the cells in the heading and subheading rows, and size the table to fit the contents. Remember to use the degree symbol in the temperature column.

Chill

Compose four bullet points that address why food must be kept cold and the proper methods of refrigeration. Title this slide (Slide 11) **Chill Know-how** and use a Title and Text slide.

C. Review Materials

You decide to create a short quiz for your employees to review what they've learned from your presentation. This is followed by a Questions slide which concludes your presentation.

1. The Questions slide is first in a series of four slides. See Figure 1 for the slide contents. Title this slide **Quiz** (Slide 12). It is a Title and Text slide, but change the bullets to numbers. Add a hyperlink to each set of Yes/No or True/False answers which will link to the appropriate answer slide shown in Figure 2.

FIGURE 1   Quiz Questions

Question Number	Question Text
1	Should hot food be placed directly in the refrigerator? Yes or No?
2	Refrigeration prevents bacterial growth. True or False?
3	It is mandatory for all employees to wash their hands after entering the restroom. Yes or No?

2. Create the three slides (Slides 13–15) that provide the answers to the quiz.

- Layout should be Title Only. Title these slides **Question One Answer**, **Question Two Answer**, and **Question Three Answer**.
- Insert text boxes on each slide and supply one answer per slide (see Figure 2 for answer text). Format the font as 32-point Arial bold.
- Change the shape of the text box to a rounded rectangle. Insert a different custom color line around each text box.
- Change the fill of the text box: for Answer 1, use Bouquet fill effect; for Answer 2, use Blue Tissue Paper fill effect; and for Answer 3, use Water Droplets fill effect.

FIGURE 2   Answers to Quiz Questions

Question Number	Slide Number	Answer Text
1	13	Yes, but divide large quantities of food into shallow containers for quicker cooling.
2	14	False. Refrigeration slows, but does not prevent the growth of harmful bacteria.
3	15	Yes. All employees must wash their hands after entering the restroom.

3. Add interactivity to the quiz by incorporating action buttons.

- For Slides 13–14, use an action button that returns the viewer to the quiz questions (Slide 12). Insert the square blank action button in the lower-right corner of the slide and format the action button so that it is 1" x 1" in size. Hyperlink the button to Slide 12. Inside the button, type **Return to Quiz**, and format the text as 12-point Arial bold.
- For Slide 15, add an action button that takes the viewer to the conclusion of the presentation (Slide 16). Format the action button as on the previous slides, but change the button text to **Continue with Presentation**.

4. Title the last slide of the presentation **Questions**, and select the Title only design. Include the text **If you have questions about Safe Food Handling Techniques, please ask your supervisor or me** in a rounded rectangular callout. Format this slide appropriately by changing the font, font size, and adding color to the callout.

D. Prepare the Slide Show

You will now make the presentation more interesting.

1. Add the Ellipse Motion animation to all slides. Run the slide show to review in preparation of your presentation to employees.

E. Share the Presentation

You are attending the local chamber of commerce meeting next week and you've offered to share this presentation with other restaurant owners. Since you're not actually giving the presentation at the meeting, you've decided to prepare a handout and make the presentation available on the chamber's Web site.

1. Add a footer to your presentation that includes the restaurant name, page number, and the credit line **Information from www. foodsafety.gov**.

2. Save the presentation as **foodsafety.htm**.

3. Print out one copy of the presentation as handouts (six slides per page) in black and white.

PROJECT RESULTS |

Upon completing this project you should have:

FranksMexicanRestaurant.ppt
FranksMexicanRestaurant.htm
FranksMexicanRestaurant_files folder